THE BHAGAVAD GĪTĀ

THE BHAGAVAD GĪTĀ

translated and introduced by
Antonio de Nicolás

NICOLAS-HAYS, INC.
York Beach, Maine

First published in 1990 by
Nicolas-Hays, Inc.
Box 612
York Beach, Maine 03910

Distributed to the trade by
Samuel Weiser, Inc.
Box 612
York Beach, Maine 03910

Library of Congress Cataloging in Publication Data
Bhagavadgītā. English.
Bhagavad Gītā / [translated by] Antonio de Nicolás.
I. De Nicolás, Antonio T., 1932– . II. Title.
BL1138.62.E5 1990
294.5′924—dc20 89-77693
CIP

ISBN 0-89254-018-4
CCP

Cover illustration is from *The Cultural Heritage of India* by Sri Ramakrishna Centenary Committee, Belur Math, Calcutta.

Printed in the United States of America

CONTENTS

Part 1

Part 2

Part 1

Introduction to *The Bhagavad Gītā*

INTRODUCTION

When reading the *Bhagavad Gītā*, it is probably helpful for Westerners to know something about its historical background. Sometime around the 12th century B.C., a great war occurred in what is now the Karnal district of Hariana State in northern India. This war involved a large number of small regional kingdoms. The historical records are not complete, so the varied and complex issues that precipitated the conflict are, and perhaps will always be, matters for speculation and dispute. Undoubtedly, the legend has grown and much has been added to the tenuous historical data, but whatever the particular elements of this complex event may have been, it is, in any case, fairly certain that a war of major proportions did occur, and that it had most serious subsequent political consequences for India. Hindus have for centuries regarded this war as a crisis point in their civilization.

Several centuries later—perhaps between the fifth and second centuries B.C.—the author of the *Gītā* used this historical event as the setting for what to his view was a basic human conflict. The final revision of the work was made during the Gupta period (fourth to seventh centuries, A.D.). One of the earliest manuscript sources dates back to Śaṃkara's commentary on the *Gītā* in the ninth century, and though a Kashmir text is believed to be somewhat earlier, the differences between the two are minimal.

The *Gītā* forms a small part—seven hundred stanzas—of the epic of the Mahābhārata—two hundred thousand lines that are contained in chapters 23 to 40 of the *Bhisma-Parvam*.

When reading the *Gītā*, we must be aware that the whole book is about Arjuna's crisis and its resolution. The author of the *Gītā* takes, therefore, a concrete man—a prince, politician, leader, warrior—in a concrete historico-cultural setting—a battle—and identifies a crisis as the starting point of the book. Arjuna's crisis arises because he identifies himself with his actions. He believes himself to be the actor and is caught in the results of his actions. It will take eighteen chapters to resolve this impasse.

With this in mind, we should not try to read the words of the *Gītā* literally. To take the words literally would be to fall into the same misconception of identification that led Arjuna to his crisis, for we might possibly misunderstand the actual concepts of hope, faith, charity, and even crisis and despair.

Here is the first clue to *not* reading the *Gītā* literally: observe how the author presents the story—anonymously. The author remains unknown (though it is speculated that his name was Vyasa), thus he doesn't identify himself with his work. The whole story is narrated by Saṃjaya, the charioteer, to his *blind* king, Dhṛtarāṣṭra. Saṃjaya hears the story in the battlefield, and it consists of a dialogue between Arjuna and his charioteer, Kṛṣṇa. Thus the author—whoever he was—brings to his own narrative the same message of the *Gītā*: beware of self-identifications.

Furthermore, Indian literature is divided into two types: *smṛti* (remembered, or interpreted), and *śruti* (literally, "what has been heard"). The author of the *Gītā*, through Arjuna's crisis, brings together both traditions in a living message. Arjuna's reconciliation between śruti and smṛti is grounded in his crisis and its resolution. Kṛṣṇa is the voice that brings and holds these worlds together. As the story develops, we find that any identification of Kṛṣṇa with his first person speech is sheer idolatry and contrary to the story of the *Gītā* itself.

For the *Gītā* to have meaning, it must appear in its own context and structure—it should not be identified as something, a book or a doctrine, which is already known to us. We must start with the *Gītā's* own initial situation: the human crisis of self-identity. This is Arjuna's concrete situation in the *Gītā*—a situation which we human beings, in order to survive, must also consider at some time or another. We need to discover how our convictions function in our lives—a function so important that unless it is recovered, we cannot act. Our challenge is not only to save Arjuna, but also the culture that gave us Arjuna.

The Body of Crisis

There is no more dramatic document in Hindu tradition than the *Bhagavad Gītā*, and the crisis and emancipation of

Arjuna, the warrior, as narrated in it. A man, a culture, need to be saved so that we, through this symbolic action, can also come to know our own preconceived notions of reality, and can become our own ground. This document, moreover, is early enough to provide us with insight into the multiple perspectives of a single culture.

Arjuna's crisis, as described in chapter 1 of the *Gītā*, is apparently a crisis about his decision to fight or not to fight. That would be fine if, indeed, Arjuna had a choice of either! Arjuna is no ordinary person—a complete social system hangs on his decision. Generations of warriors before him, and his own thirteen years in exile, have made him ready for what is facing him now in the field of battle, the "field of *dharma*." Or have they? Apparently not. Sin and guilt wrap around him and threaten to submerge him in a sea of despair. In fact, Arjuna's body is so heavy with sin and guilt that it inevitably sinks into an almost catatonic inaction.

Regardless of the merits of war and peace, Arjuna's crisis is radically grounded in three basic presuppositions:

1) There is a body and only one body belonging to Arjuna to which the attributes of crisis (sin, guilt, despair, etc.) can be ascribed;

2) It is this belief or presupposition that decides Arjuna's course of action or inaction, and his crisis and despair; and

3) This is a kind of radical knowledge that grounds Arjuna's crisis—it is the basic orientation which makes the crisis possible.

These presuppositions, and the host of others they bring along—language, reality, the metaphysical hierarchy of absolute forms, eternal truths, ideas in the mind—might not even make us blink. This is how we, too, are accustomed to "seeing" things and ourselves. However, it is just such an abstract theory that catapults us out of the experienced world by draining it of meaning, throwing us into the arms of existentialism, despair, and the psychiatric couch. These preconceived notions, all that we take for granted as "real," are what catapult the self—and Arjuna—into crisis.

Much of the *Gītā* is lost in interpretation by not paying attention to the first chapter and the clues it provides for both Arjuna's crisis and the path of its eventual resolution. We need to focus on the movement of the first chapter as the basis of its kinesthetic, or dynamic, orientation. Only then can we retrieve the context through which its action gains meaning. From Arjuna's viewpoint, his orientation is the metaphysical unity between himself and the action confronting him. His decision about the way things are makes him dependent on the result of his actions.

The first chapter clusters names upon names and adjectives upon adjectives. There are the names of warriors, kings, relatives, gurus, men and animals, weapons, musical instruments, bows, rewards and punishments. There is also a concomitant list of adjectives, properties, descriptions, decisions, indecisions, and so forth, attributable to those names. We might even believe that the Sanskrit language has no verbs, or that their function has been purposely stopped, at least for the time being.

Arjuna's crisis orients itself toward this cluster of names and properties and their permanence or destruction in the battlefield. These names and their properties weigh so heavily that Arjuna cannot see himself as anything but a name with properties—an agent, an actor, a body upon which the weight of all these names and properties lean—until he is crushed into inaction.

It is this abstraction that drains Arjuna's world of all meaning and leads him to crisis. It is such a context that structures Arjuna's body into a body of sadness, sorrow, weakness; a body that trembles, whose hair stands on end, whose mouth dries up, who can barely stand, mind reeling, skin burning.

In our search for meaning we also must not saddle the interpretation of the *Gītā* with the names of Arjuna and Kṛṣṇa, or we will also be forced to mount the hidden horses—the abstract theory of names—that so much of our Western tradition carries with it. We take possession by names—we know things by our experience of them, by their quantifiable sense-data, the qualities or characteristics cluttered around them, the abstract concepts that the mind applies to things or names, subjects facing objects, things moving in space and linear time, thinking substances facing matter, fallen bodies facing heaven, what is and what ought to be.

The Body of Sound

Arjuna's search for meaning, together with our own, will have to move through seventeen chapters of exercises. First we get clues as to the direction of the search. Then we see a difference in perspective between Arjuna and Kṛṣṇa. We see Kṛṣṇa's perspective in chapter 11. And then there is the world of sound. Beyond Arjuna's crisis, and underlying Kṛṣṇa's and Arjuna's moves within the culture, there is a whole world of sound and movement that makes these moves possible. This sound-movement-world is what, in the words of St. John of the Cross, we may call "the sounding silence," in which the world of the *Gītā* is submerged, and which we must recover if we are to give the *Gītā* its own meaning.

Think of it: this whole interaction between Arjuna and Kṛṣṇa is overheard in battle—over the roars of men, the tumultuous sounds of conch shells blowing, kettledrums, cymbals and horns, amid the clanging of armor, weapons, chariots, amid the nervous excitement of animals and people—through all this the author is able to hear a *whispered* dialogue! The *Gītā's* body stretches as far as its voice is heard.

Arjuna's surrender of his life to meaninglessness is the result of his decision about a knowledge that is absolute and his decision about a body that is also absolute. The path that Kṛṣṇa will force Arjuna to follow in search of emancipation will be an effort to correct this initial absolute and objective illusion.

Where Arjuna will rely for his identification on the *ahaṃkāra* (the I-maker), Kṛṣṇa will propose the *anahaṃ*vādīn (not the "I" speaking) as the linguistic modality of dwelling in the world. Where Arjuna relies on the *manas* interpretation of sensation, Kṛṣṇa will propose the *buddhi* interpretation, with its contextual dependence, rather than the absolutized form of sensation repeated by the *manas* interpretation. Where Arjuna's moves rely on his own thought, Kṛṣṇa will show him the absolute emptiness of his moves by making him realize the circumstantial moves within which thought, knowledge, and body are already moving and expressing their moves within the situation facing them.

In the same way that Arjuna doesn't understand Kṛṣṇa, we should also consider the presuppositions forced on us by our own English language. We need to be aware that our metaphors to describe memories are linear—covered with words like river, stream, chain, train. This linear thinking reinforces the belief in a theoretical consciousness that remains constant. It cannot account for the circumstances we face in every action without reducing them to a theory—but a theory that in no way changes our assumptions about memory, consciousness or the body. Linear thinking underlies all our methods of induction and deduction and distributive logic, along with all their distributive laws of and/or.

Cause and effect are similarly connected. In the same way, we trace the *path* of a statistical graph, a historical development, a personal biography, the evolution from ape to mystic. Motivation and response follow the same linear path, and so does thought, action, life, reason, argument, conversation, and the path of salvation. Our language cannot function without the and/or connections, and our very language reinforces our reductionist tendencies both in relation to our experience and in relation to other people's cultures.

Yet how ironic that the contemporary quantum logic of modern physics is a nonlinear, nondistributive, intertwining lattice of sentences where the distributive laws—the and/or—have been dropped. Still, the linear logic of our language has not yet made room for the nonlinear character of human experience.

Unless we have this in mind, the moves of the *Gītā* will be difficult to see. These moves are nonlinear in character in the sense that each of them is in a complete situation in itself: a body totally oriented toward a cultural origin, aperspectival and bodiless, which becomes perspective and flesh simultaneously with every human move. *Puruṣa* and *Prakṛti*, vision and interpretation, Kṛṣṇa and Arjuna, function in the *Gītā* as the embodiment of these generalizations.

The Body in Training

Simultaneous with Arjuna's form of knowledge, there is Kṛṣṇa's—a knowledge that not only includes reflection, but is a *form* of reflection, fed by the multiplicity of social regional ontologies and their perspectives as they surround both Kṛṣṇa and Arjuna. It is, moreover, a knowledge intentionally directed toward the recovery of its own original orientation, the absolute present. The *Gītā* speaks of time in only two senses: one is the present, the now; the rest is memory. Chapter 11 makes it dramatically clear: "*Kalo'smi*," or literally, "Time am I." This is the absolute present; the rest is memories, embodied memories of other presents built of the dark and terrifying present, the present that we so anxiously avoid.

Arjuna's and Kṛṣṇa's consciousness—plus their radical original orientation—form the necessary conditions for the culture—the *Gītā*—to be. All three have to be accounted for. Any one of them made absolute would be no culture at all; at least, not the culture of the *Gītā*.

The integration of multiple perspectives is not possible if ultimately knowledge is not mediated through a radical sacrifice of perspectives. It is through this sacrifice that human knowing as an embodied vision may be opened up, and the multiplicity of actual human spaces for interaction and communication may be made possible and experienced. In this way, the originating aperspectival ground, which made possible the subsequent multiplicity, may be recovered.

When anyone is in the midst of a crisis, like Arjuna's, things must first get worse before they get better; the crisis must reach bottom before it is resolved. Arjuna's initial condition in the *Gītā* is a complete blank. He is *tamas*, dullness and inertia. It is not the case that Arjuna "feels" lows. Rather it is the case that Arjuna *is* the whole *tamasic* condition, not only in his mind but in his whole body-feelings-sensation. If Arjuna had been able, in his moment of crisis, to realize that his body was as large as his tamasic condition; if he had been able to realize the dependence of body-feelings on perspective and realize also this metaphysical unity, then the subsequent journey of the *Gītā* would have been superfluous. But Arjuna, like most of us, settles instead for a crisis, and the *Gītā's* wheel goes on.

Arjuna's crisis and despair can be read from chapters 1 through 11 of the *Gītā*. Kṛṣṇa's resolution of this crisis, his own dependence on Arjuna and their simultaneous moves can be seen through chapters 2 to 10 and 12 to 18. Chapter 11 will appear in the *Gītā* as the absolute present mediating and grounding the moves of the past and the future, Arjuna's and Kṛṣṇa's.

The structure of the journey between chapters 2 and 10 is a structure to be "seen" in order to be understood. Through a mediation of memory—the lived memories of Arjuna's past, the imaginative variations of a life lived and forgotten—Arjuna is able to re-feel his body as it felt and thought in different contexts. This is Sāṃkhya and Yoga: Karmayoga—the yoga of action; Jñānayoga—the yoga of knowledge; Karmasaṃnyasayoga—the yoga of meditation; Jñānavijñānayoga—the yoga of wisdom and understanding; Akṣarabrahmayoga—the yoga of imperishable Brahman; Rājavidyaṛajaguhyayoga—the yoga of sovereign knowledge and sovereign secret; and Vibhūtiyoga—the yoga of manifestation. Within each of these contexts, world-body-feelings are different; the motivation of each context determines actions and the way these actions world-body-feel.

This long journey of lost memories is a journey of re-embodiment for a man who has been reduced to inaction and impotence. We must understand that it is a journey that is grounded in the realization that a reference for language, perception, or experience in general does not exist. But the conclusion of such a journey of re-embodiment shows the futility of trying to grasp at anything permanent. Chapter 11 shows the finality, dissolution, and despair of any world that is grounded in permanence.

What we see in this journey is that Arjuna's memories are lived memories. He has experienced them and therefore knows how they world-body-feel. Arjuna is able to body-feel his own body while traveling the corridors of his memories. He is able to body-feel other body-feelings he himself was when those memories were *not* memories, but a living body. He knows of other world-unions that are possible through himself, or that he, himself, has been.

But for anyone on such a journey, these body-unions are problematic. We may decide to ascribe all these memories, all these imaginative variations, to the same constant body. That is, we may ascribe them to a body that remains constant through all these variations and to which memories—imaginative variations—are never recoverable as embodied, but are only possible as embodied attributes from a logical world to a logical subject. This union is a precarious one, a theoretic unity to which different sensations, different body-feelings may be ascribed, or may be denied. We can never find ourselves at home in such a body. And the only way out is either to declare ourselves in crisis—go crazy—or diligently dedicate ourselves to the task of finding our own emancipation.

Since the *Gītā* continues, we take it that Arjuna decides for emancipation rather than crisis, but by this decision alone, we find that he has already changed. Faith is no longer anything or any god, but rather a space beyond any god. Knowledge is no longer the absolutized universal knowledge that led him into crisis, but rather, "Know me, O Bhārata, to be the knower of the field in every field; the knowledge of the field and of the knower of the field; this I hold to be (real) knowledge." The body will appear as a radical embodied unity, a multiplicity of body-feelings-sensations, complete each time it acts, in every action, in every social situation. But the body also must retrain itself—"re-member"—every time its acts require not only time, but also the constant effort and habit of learning how to shift perspectives—a 180 degree turn in every action.

The metaphysical clues to this path of recovery are found in the knowledge (liberating action knowledge) that action (*karman*) belongs to *dharma*:

Dharma to the situation or guṇas;
The Gunas to prakṛti (body-interpretations);
Prakṛti to puruṣa (embodied vision);
Puruṣa manifests itself through prakṛti,
which acts through the guṇas,
which act through dharma,
which acts through karman.

All human actions and their knowledge are woven of the larger fabric of the *yugas*, the cosmic guṇas from which we create our world (nonattached action-knowledge) or our crisis (attached action-knowledge). Our circumstance, to be saved, has to find its creative situation in the constantly moving world around it. We (and our world) are in constant change and movement. Attached thought-action either stops us or the world in its actual course.

The Body of Karma

Kṛṣṇa's mode of action-knowledge in the *Gītā* is the prototype of the unattached and dedicated path to find our creative liberation. Kṛṣṇa's mode of acting in the world is the prototype of an activity that lets life pass through us without breaking its rhythm or its flow because of self-made or self-appropriated thought-body-actions.

Liberated people, like Kṛṣṇa, have a necessary and sufficient condition to save our circumstance—to know the field in every field. Of this knowledge new worlds are made. But Kṛṣṇa could not save any world, any body, if Arjuna—prakṛti, the body—could not "re-member itself up" to the embodied vision every action demands of both Kṛṣṇa and Arjuna. They are metaphysical equals, and inseparable.

Some people claim that the *Gītā* is repetitious and could have well ended with chapter 13. It is easy to understand why such a claim has been made. Faith and knowledge, as presented in chapters 12 and 13, are attributed to a god in whose love knowledge and faith find their fulfillment. But to the degree that such an interpretation of the *Gītā* gives life to the text of the *Gītā*, it also disembodies the world by denying it in its flesh. Neither faith nor knowledge in the *Gītā* rest on such theoretic solutions to the human problem. What these theoretic interpretations miss is the sophisticated understanding and development of the human body that the *Gītā* represents.

No matter how we choose to interpret the *Gītā*, nothing will change it. Arjuna will still go into crisis. His knowledge will still be reduced to some form of theoretic synthesis, his liberation will still be reduced to a fruitless hope that somebody—someone else besides him—might be able to pull him out of the situation he himself is incapable of understanding.

This is the world of *saṃsāra*—birth and death, origin and dissolution—because the knowledge that holds it together is not only disembodied, but it is not even capable of "seeing itself." Or to put it differently, what this knowledge sees is not its own movements, but rather the crystalized, static, stagnant repetitions of a structure that takes its own ground for granted. This is the reason why, regardless of how many lives we live, how many memories we have—even while we talk of maturity, change, growth, and of being different—we keep being reborn again and again into the same kind of body. This is the world of saṃsāra. The round of birth and death is only possible when we systematically lobotomize the living flesh for a theoretic substitute that remains constant in spite of the multiplicity of body-world-changes through which we play out our lives.

When we "see" as Kṛṣṇa does, then neither the world nor the self nor ourselves are what Arjuna thinks them to be. All there is is movement—fleeting, changing, speeding up or slowing down. And unless we learn to see the movement, hear its sound, dance on its rhythmic waves, we have no alternative than to stop the world and triumphantly call the movement of thought the movement of the world. When we do this, human pain, human crisis, and human despair are born.

But the *Gītā* does not propose that we substitute one world for the other, nor proclaim one better than the other. The human condition is such that both worlds make up human life. Either we learn to live with both or we will remain forever incomplete. Both worlds are of equal value and both worlds depend on one another. Their interrelationship, however, is radical. What can truly be said in one cannot be truly said in the other. Understanding this type of complementary relationship is shared by modern physics and applies not only to two separate worlds, but to every action if we take it in its circumstantial completeness—i.e., an action-body situation.

Kṛṣṇa's dependence on Arjuna, or the puruṣa's dependence on prakṛti—vision's dependence of perspective on the body. Without this dependence and complementarity, the moves of the *Gītā* would make no sense. It is the movement of the puruṣa through the multiple prakṛtic situations in search of its own embodied liberation. In this sense, any statement that can truly be affirmed in one context—or action-body—is only true in relation to those conditions, and is also limited by those same conditions. The same statement cannot be true in another situation (or prakṛtic condition), nor can the same statement be true even if the same conditions appear to be identically duplicated. No human situation is repeatable, even for the same body.

Kṛṣṇa's moves—as we see from chapters 3 through 18—are intentional moves for a very definite purpose: the emancipation of Arjuna. This emancipation is not possible unless Arjuna is desensitized from the one way of body-feeling-sensing he has reduced himself to by way of the *manas*-interpretation of sensation. That desensitization depends on detachment. Our concern here, then, is to clarify how Kṛṣṇa's moves lead to detachment and emancipation through successive desensitizations and resensitizations.

What Kṛṣṇa actually performs for Arjuna is the multiplication, the dismemberment, of Arjuna's own body as it really embodied itself through other orientations, other memories, and sensed itself embodied as such distinct bodies. Chapters 2 through 10 contain the journey of such an embodied movement, a dance of prolonged frequency and low intensity, high and low pitched, but with one conclusion in mind. Arjuna is not the body he believes himself to be: he is also the multiplicity of bodies he has been through in his memories; all these bodies are alive and asking for release from Arjuna's prostrated and depressed body facing the battlefield.

In trying to understand the *Gītā*, we have to bear in mind all the previous action the *Gītā* has forced Arjuna to perform on his own view of the circumstance around him—and on himself. We have to bear in mind that Arjuna has touched his own emptiness (chapter 11), the absolute bereavement of what he took to be the solid ground of his body-feelings, and that new lenses have been put before his eyes, new auditory devices have been put on his ears, and that for Arjuna, the world cannot be seen or heard in the same old way again. The very structure of Arjuna's meaning has changed forever. The same has happened to the text of the *Gītā*.

The strangeness of the new situation demands a critical change, not only in conceptual structures, but also in relearning of the new process of body-feeling, a re-education of the muscular and nervous systems, and above all a change in the conceptual structure that will account for the new situation. This is the change, during which a whole new style of embodied interpretation is assembled, but this is not achieved without an intellectual bereavement. This can only proceed to relearn its own process of formation step by step, action by action—how to walk, sit, fight, perform rituals, interact with others, talk, sing, dance, even eat leftovers. For those who know, who act on the radical orientation of chapter 11, every action is dangerous, for each one contains the creation and the dissolution of the world.

Every spot in Arjuna's world is now explosive, for in it the whole creation is present. "It is the upturned peepal tree, with its branches below, its roots above. The branches stretch below and above, nourished by the guṇas, its sprouts are the sense objects. When this tree reaches the world, it spreads out its roots that result in action." But we do not see how their actions are so umbilically joined to the whole world. "They do not comprehend its form, nor its end, nor its beginning, nor its foundation. Their only way out is to cut their firmly rooted tree with the weapon of nonattachment. Only those who have the eye of wisdom are able to see that it is only a fraction of the grounding self which appears as a living eternal self, and draws into its power the five senses and the mind that comes from prakṛti; but taking or leaving a body, they take all these along, like the wind carrying perfume from a home. They enjoy the objects of the senses, using the ear, eye, touch, smell and the mind." But we have to distinguish puruṣa from prakṛti, perspective and body. "This is the vision the yogins see in their own self, but the mindless, whose self is not ready yet, even if they strive, they do not see."

Arjuna should not only be a warrior in name, but he should learn to live as a warrior. And among the plural conditions that make up a warrior, the most important one is waiting patiently for the right condition to act. Take a piece of land and there will be as many perspectives as people passing through it. But for a warrior, every piece of land is all the life there is. In fact, there is only every single action for him to count on as "his life" as a warrior, and it is in every action that he will throw himself with the full power of his decisions. A warrior's life is a life of a strategy about every action, and among those actions he has to discover also the strategy of waiting for the right action.

For a warrior, everything is mortally dangerous. A trap hides behind every door, every bush, every branch; but in order to be trapped, a warrior must be willing. He must be willing not to be a warrior, and to abandon his will to be a warrior to his desire to be less than a warrior.

From chapter 16 to 18, Arjuna's journey to recover his will—to "do as you desire"—includes also the capacity to wait and stall for the right conditions. "For there are those who, without patience, throw themselves to the pursuit of pleasure on the excuse that there is no truth in the world. These are people lost in themselves, small in mind, cruel in deed, enemies of the world. They surrender to desire, arrogance, and hypocrisy, and they justify themselves with false philosophies. They only cling to what leads to death, they strive for wealth to gratify their desires; and they can only speak in the first person: I have won today; that desire I will obtain; this is mine; this wealth will become mine; I am lord and enjoyer; I am perfect, strong and happy; I am wealthy, well-born; I will sacrifice; I will give; I will rejoice, who else is like me?" The destiny of these people is to be born again under the same conditions that perpetuate their delusions in every action. These people do not have enough faith to be able to wait. For we should be able to act in every situation as the situation acts on itself—without self-appropriations.

Arjuna's conclusion, at the end of his long journey, is to realize his own emancipation through the action facing him. Through that action, Kṛṣṇa, Arjuna, puruṣa, prakṛti, and their orienting foundation coincide. For emancipation to be possible, however, Arjuna's will has to coincide with the original cultural will of which both Kṛṣṇa and Arjuna are the body. But this realization could not have been mediated had Arjuna not been able to re-member himself.

In the search for meaning, it would be a great oversight if we did not at least sketch the conditions of possibility for recovery of the cultural will of the tradition with which we are dealing. The conditions of possibility are not themselves the experience. It is really up to the readers to embody the circumstance by being able to "hear" what Arjuna constantly thinks he "sees."

Our Bodies

There are two radical experiences I owe to India and which the translation of this book has forced me to re-embody. One is the problematic notion itself of the body, which through my life in India became so many other bodies. The other is the model of music I discovered through Indian chant, music, and language. It is this latter model of music that allowed me to make sense of a body that was already moving according to a rhythm that only now I have begun to understand. Before I learned any Indian languages, or any cultural theories about Indian life, my body was already, in its silent way, drawing different bodily structures. I chanted before I learned to speak, and somehow, even without my knowing it, my body was silently shedding a multiplicity of perspectives of itself—made possible through the constant variation in perspectives induced through the musical activity.

I did not then understand, and I am only now beginning to glimpse, the relationship between the two experiences—the body and music. It is a great failure in our educational system that music is no longer a formal part of the curriculum, but it is, nonetheless, clear to me now why in many civilizations, including ours, music was considered the grounding of both training and education. It is also quite clear to me now the role of music in Plato's thought, and his need to "let the musicians in and spoil the order of the banquet" after his careful discursive arguments of the Symposium. If we could only "see" all that they "hear."

Returning to India, the search for meaning would be incomplete and our recovery of the cultural will impossible, if we did not at least consider that the cultural moves we observe in the *Gītā* will not gain full meaning unless the theory of the body, as I have developed it here, finds its correspondence in the theory of music. It is obvious that this theory of music is not fully developed in the *Gītā*, though it is fully presupposed. It goes back to the Ṛg Veda and the Brahmanas. It is the theory underlying Ṛta and Vṛtra, Indra and Agni, the Puruṣa Sukta and Prajāpati, embodiment and dismemberment.

Contrary to our Cartesian and linear way of understanding the mind-body relationship and problem, the *Gītā* forces us to face the same relationship and problem from a totally opposite perspective. In fact, 180 degrees different. While from a Western perspective we are used to conceiving the mind-body relationship as two opposing substances, where the mind has the upper hand, control, and direction of the body, the *Gītā* offers us instead a body—field or prakṛti—which, in order to act, finds in every action a perspective—puruṣa—or a radical interpretation of itself as it encounters it. Of this body-perspective-appropriation, the whole journey of the *Gītā* is undertaken.

The *Gītā* moves on music. Every action is to be understood as modelled on a sound-point or tone. As a sound-point, every action is both a limit and an origin of manifestation: the "male" principle symbolized by an integer "cutting" the undifferentiated pitch continuum, thus opening space itself—the "female" principle—to further differentiation.

Much of the mystery surrounding Hindu thought and practice could be erased, especially in the later tantric tradition, if these musical and mathematical ideas would be thoroughly examined. When projecting integer arithmetic into a tone-circle—linking the female matrix with the continuum of real numbers—it is obvious that the matrix cannot be divided and subdivided into equal parts. Thus we are continually confronted with imperfection and "uncleanliness." This is also the reason why no mantra is chantable; we can only chant one *kind* of mantra or another. There is no ground for any form of absolutism or dogmatism.

It is on this understanding of sound-point that space and time may be understood as both the occasion and the challenge for a complete embodiment in every action. For it is on every sound-point that the whole body-perspective plays out its whole human life—its manifestation and dissolution. The world is created and destroyed in every action.

The complete embodied vision which the *Gītā* proposes to us in every action is not possible unless the body and its appropriated perspective is systematically trained in an activity that would enable the body to shed its appropriated perspective as it moves from sound-point to sound-point in the scale. The body-movement and embodied vision is implied in a "tuning-theory" that tries to reconcile a multitude of alternate perspectives of the tonefield and the related number field without reducing it to one system. We should be aware that numbers, in the sense of rational numbers—restricted as they are to integers—are inadequate to completely define the continuum of the octave. More specifically, any division of the octave cycle in equal parts (meaning parts in proportion, in the same ratio) is arithmetically impossible, and requires the later concept of real number. Any system of tuning requires that some ideal value be sacrificed at some point in the cycle. The fact that the Hindus do not mathematize their scales in the Greek way suggests that they have always known—even from Ṛg Vedic times—this lesson.

Music, unlike our English language, is nonlinear. And in this sense perhaps it is the key to understanding the nonlinear moves of the *Gītā*.

We have all referred to the cultural voice, or the cultural will, to orient our own search for meaning. In this sense, music provides a model and ground for meaning. The moves of the *Gītā* are not only descriptive, but normative—they agree with the tradition that has been proclaimed from the Ṛg Veda down as an exact form of acting (*satya, ṛta*). The Hindu musician takes his stand on any pitch: that is, Hindu theory of music is a theory of relative, not absolute pitch, and what is even more important, it achieves a wide range of modal tunings only because it is acutely sensitive to the precise values of pure octaves, fifths, and thirds. These form an inner metric space which make it possible to deviate from them by one or two "quarter-tones," the least perceptively different pitch intervals. Octaves, fifths and thirds, are true norms, part of all our psychoacoustical equipment. These are culturally reinforced in Hinduism, and, significantly, repressed (i.e., the pure third is repressed) in all countries of the West, where equal-temperament is imperialistically elevated to the status of "cultural norm."

It is obvious that the notion of cultural norm plays a profound role in the *Gītā*, permeated through norms of diversity. Arjuna is a man in search of full-embodiment, which implies that he must carry with him into battle (or any action) the social and cultural norms around him. It is only in this normative sense that Arjuna's action is equally essential to friends and enemies. It is for this reason that the Hindu world of the *Gītā* depends on Arjuna for its survival, on the condition that through Arjuna, the cultural norms of the *Gītā* find a living body, an incarnation, to keep its wheel moving.

• • •

I would like to conclude these meditations through the *Bhavagad Gītā* with some general reflections. The beginning of our journey focused on the systematic effort of an individual, Arjuna, to surrender to nonmovement in a moment of crisis. This impossible effort was mediated by a reflection on the frightening discovery that the soil upon which we stand is never secure. It has to be renewed again and again in every action. Even the appearance of nonmovement is a tension begotten by movement and destined to fall apart in order to give way to new movement, which then creates new tensions, new worlds. Movement speaks out of the body-perspective of all things. Crisis in the *Gītā* is the triggering mechanism of one individual's effort to discover the orienting context that dictates his body movement. The *Gītā* makes it amply clear that it is through the discovery of these body-movement-orientations that we may create our own emancipation, and our own world. We can avoid the self-strangulation and desensitization of repeating the same conceptual and absolute body-movement-scheme to death.

Underlying the *Gītā* there is only one reason offered for this eternal cycle of crisis, reflection, and embodied vision: faith. This faith, however, is not in any god, person or institution, but in human life. It is the love of life's own body. Gods, people, or institutions are this side of creation, and it is through them that human life becomes flesh, incarnate, through every renewed human presence. Life is a continuously recurring problem that we must give body through our own body-orientation. Kṛṣṇa and Arjuna are the body-perspective, the embodied vision, of their own cultural body. They are inseparable and incomplete without the cultural will and tradition that oriented their moves in the first place, and in every place. Their apparent split in the *Gītā* is only for the time being, as long as it takes for the body to think itself up to the original orientation of the culture. This lift is also a gigantic effort of love for the human body around us, and our own.

The theme of journey has forced us to strew our paths with many conceptual corpses. Our systematic effort to make reason through other people's reasons has forced us to sacrifice ideas, models, presuppositions, perspectives, all along this path. The most radical sacrifice being that only one kind of reason may be rational. We were unaware that this dehumanizing demand on what reason should be has been determining our own way of body-feeling-sensing other people for centuries. And that while we were ready to tolerate their ideas, we could only tolerate them as long as our way of body-feeling-sensing would not have to change. In a radical sense, we condemned ourselves to perpetual wandering along a path of discursive thought which could only function discursively by in the end reducing our own human body to absolute insensibility and disorientation. Our educational system, psychology, the social sciences, philosophy, and even religion, are guilty of this sin of systematic disembodiment.

The *Gītā*, on the other hand, has made us aware that underlying all classifications, all definitions, all situations (*sattva*, *rajas*, *tamas*), underlying the analytic and synthetic side of our reason (the two sides of brain, manas, buddhi), there is a body finding perspectives in every situation as it moves along.

Human life—Eastern or Western, Arjuna's or the present interpreter's—means having to deal with the world—a world. This cannot be done in the abstract, but only in the concrete situation of an individually felt vital need that fills us with the anxiety of life in a moment of crisis. This perception of anxiety is unique to each of us. The concepts by which we think cannot be found ready-made, but must be extracted for the circumstantial architecture of our world. If the concepts by which we think are not capable of embodying the circumstantial architecture of the world, then we are condemned by the hand of our own limited and distorted vision to surrender to the fate of others, to be a slave of circumstances, to inaction—crisis.

The occasion for Arjuna's crisis is the fact that he is in a battle situation. The crisis is Arjuna's own identification of himself with his actions, unaware of the fact that this decision about this identification is not part of the battle: on the contrary, it is the willing reduction of Arjuna, the warrior, the leader, to a vision of himself short of his tradition and his training that reduces him to inaction. The battle is not the issue in Arjuna's crisis, but rather Arjuna's decision about himself in this battle situation that is at issue. His problem is none other than his identification with his action—taking unto himself literally the identity of the grammatical "I."

It would be a grave misreading of the *Gītā* to make an issue of the abstract values for or against war. To take such an abstract stand would be to misread from the beginning the whole intentionality of the *Gītā*. Nor would its message change because Arjuna fights with chariots and arrows, and we have thermonuclear weapons hanging over our heads. We are not dealing here with possible wars. We are dealing in human possibilities. What is at issue is how we, as readers, decide to see ourselves in *our* critical situations. What makes us falter, doubt, stop on the path? What leads us to despair, inaction, abandonment, when faced with a determined crisis? What kind of people are we to helplessly abandon ourselves to fate, or chance—even despair?

If we—as Arjuna in this case—are seriously concerned with this problem, we will find the activity (truth) that will quiet our anxiety. We will develop a disciplined commitment (personal morality) to carry out this program of soothing radical needs. When a problem is as vitally felt as Arjuna's, neither truth nor ethics are in any way a conformity to already established norms of thought or behavior. For truth and ethics are the necessary acts and habits of those in search of freedom. They are the habits and acts of those in need to invent themselves anew, to remake themselves.

The difficulty of human life is that it is not given to anyone ready-made. Like it or not, human life is a series of instant decisions, one after the other, like the moves on a chessboard.

At each moment it is necessary to make up our minds about what we are going to do next. In order to decide what to do next, we are compelled to have a plan of what we are supposed to do, or resort to some plan someone else has made for us. It is not the case that we should make a plan. There is simply no possible life, sublime or mean, wise or stupid, that is not characterized by its preceeding according to some plan. Read chapters 16 through 18, for example; even if we abandon our lives to chance in a moment of crisis—like Arjuna proposes to do in chapter 1—we are really making a plan!

In the West, we think we choose our way in life. Actually we are interpreters, but our interpretations of ourselves and our world are not arbitrary—not even exclusively our own. Our interpretations belong to a cultural pool, or even a divine origin with which we must tune our individual wills for the continuity and the renewal of life, ours and that of the species. Arjuna's crisis is a model of what we can do or must do in a human crisis. Reading the *Gītā* should be an exercise in human liberation.

Part 2

The Bhagavad Gītā

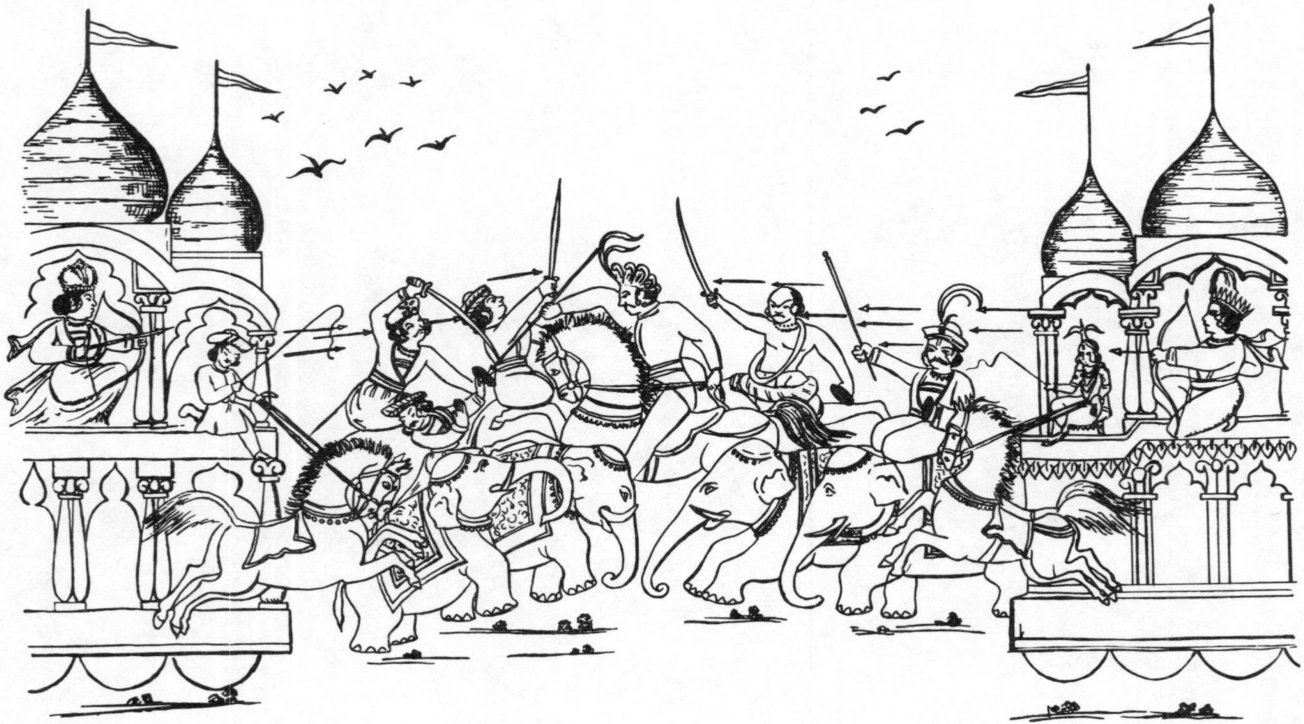

Plate 1. The battlefield. (From *Hindu Mythology* by W. J. Wilkins, London, 1882.)

Chapter 1

THE YOGA OF ARJUNA'S CRISIS

Dhṛtarāṣṭra said:

1. My sons and those of Pāṇḍu, what did they do,
Saṃjaya, when, eager to fight, they assembled
On the field of the Kurus, the field of *dharma*?

Saṃjaya said:

2. Having looked over
The Pāṇḍava troop drawn up in battle order, then
Prince Duryodhana approached his teacher (Droṇa) and spoke these words:

3. Behold, O Teacher, this great army of the sons of Pāṇḍu,
Gathered by an intelligent pupil of yours,
The son of Drupada.

4. Here are great archers who are equal in battle
To Bhīma and Arjuna, heroes like Yuyudhāna and Virāta, and Drupada,
A great chariot-warrior;

5. Together with Dhṛṣṭaketu, Cekitāna, and the courageous King of Kāśi;
Then, too, Purujit, Kuntibhoja, and Śaibya,
The best of men.

6. And then there is Yudhāmanyu the strong, and Uttamaujas the brave,
And the son of Subhadrā and the sons of Draupadī,
All of them mighty chariot-warriors.

7. O Highest of the Twice-Born,
Know also the most distinguished of our men, leaders in my army.
Let me name them for your recognition.

8. There is yourself (Droṇa), and Bhīṣma and Karṇa,
And Kṛpa victorious in battle,
Aśvatthāman and Vikarṇa, and also the son of Somadatta.

9. Many other heroes are also willing to risk their lives for my sake,
And all of them are skilled in war
And armed with many kinds of weapons.

10. Our force, however, commanded by Bhīṣma,
Appears to be unlimited
While theirs, commanded by Bhīma, appears to be small.

11. Therefore above all let all you lords,
Posted in all directions,
Support Bhīṣma.

12. To bring him (Duryodhana) joy,
The oldest grandson of the Kurus (Bhīṣma) roared loudly like a lion,
And blew his conch shell.

13. Then conches and kettledrums, cymbals and drums and horns,
All were suddenly sounded,
And the noise was tumultuous.

14. Then Mādhava (Kṛṣṇa) and the son of Pāṇḍu (Arjuna),
Both stationed in a great chariot yoked to white horses,
Blew their wondrous conches.

15. The Lord-of-the-Senses (Kṛṣṇa) blew Pāñcajanya,
Wealth-Winner (Arjuna), Devadatta,
And Bhīma, voracious, of terrible deeds, blew his great conch, Pauṇḍra.

16. Soon Prince Yudhiṣṭhira, son of Kuntī,
Was blowing Anantavijaya,

Nakula and Sahadeva were blowing Sughoṣa and Maṇipuṣpaka.

17. They were joined by the supreme archer of Kāśi,
And the great warrior Śikhaṇḍin, and Dhṛṣṭadyumna,
Virāṭa, and the invincible Sātyaki;

18. Drupada, the sons of Draupadī,
And the strong-armed son of Subhadrā:
O Lord of Earth, all these also blew their conches.

19. The tumultuous noise, resounding through heaven and earth,
Rent open the hearts of the sons of Dhṛtarāṣṭra.

20. Then, Lord of Earth, with the fighting about to begin,
The ape-bannered son of Pāṇḍu (Arjuna) seeing Dhṛtarāṣṭra's sons
Stationed in battle order, took up his bow.

21. And to Hṛṣīkeśa (Kṛṣṇa), then, O Lord of Earth,
He spoke these words:
Stop my chariot in the middle of the two armies, Unshaken one,

22. That I may behold these men standing there eager to fight,
With whom I am to engage in this war.

23. I want to see those who, about to fight, are assembled here
Desirous of accomplishing in battle
What is dear to the evil-minded son of Dhṛtarāṣṭra.

24. Thus addressed by Guḍākeśa (Arjuna), O Descendant of Bhārata (Dhṛtarāṣṭra),
Hṛṣīkeśa (Kṛṣṇa) placed the best of chariots in the middle of the two armies.

25. And when they were placed facing Bhīṣma, Droṇa and all the princes,
He said: O Son of Pṛthā (Arjuna),
Behold the assembled Kurus!

26. Arjuna saw standing there fathers and grandfathers,
Teachers, uncles, brothers, sons, grandsons, companions,

27. Fathers-in-law and friends, belonging to both armies.
And having looked closely at all these relations standing there,
The son of Kuntī (Arjuna)

28. Filled with the utmost sadness,
And weighed down by his sorrow, he said:
Kṛṣṇa, seeing my own kin on hand and eager to fight,

29. My limbs become weak, my mouth dries up,
My body trembles, and my hair stands on end.

30. Gāṇḍīva (the bow) slips from my hand;
My skin is also burning, I can scarcely remain standing;
My mind is reeling.

31. And I see bad omens, O Keśava (Kṛṣṇa),
And I forsee no good that could come from having slain my own kin in war.

32. I do not crave victory for myself, Kṛṣṇa, nor kingdom nor pleasures.
Of what use is kingdom to us, O Govinda (Kṛṣṇa)
Of what use pleasure, or even life?

33. Those for whose sake kingdom and enjoyments and pleasures we desire,
Are entering the fight
Relinquishing their lives and riches.

34. Teachers, fathers, sons, grandfathers, uncles,
Fathers-in-law, grandsons, brothers-in-law, and (other) relations:

35. Though I am slain, I do not desire to slay them. O Madhusūdana (Kṛṣṇa),
Even for the kingship of the three worlds.
Why, then, for the sake of the earth?

36. What pleasure would there be for us in slaying Dhṛtarāṣṭra's sons,
O Janārdana (Kṛṣṇa), Exciter-of-Men?

Only evil would attach to us if we slayed these (our would be) murderers.

37. Hence we ought not slay Dhṛtarāṣṭra's sons, our kinsmen;
For having slain our own kin,
How will we be happy, O Mādhava?

38. Even if they, whose minds are afflicted with greed,
Do not see the evil caused by destruction of a family
And the crime incurred in the harming of a friend;

39. Why is it not wise for us, O Janārdana (Kṛṣṇa),
Who see this evil of causing the destruction of a family,
To hold back from this sin?

40. In the ruin of a family, the ancient family *dharma* disappears,
And with the destruction of *dharma,*
Adharma overcomes the whole family.

41. When *adharma* conquers, O Kṛṣṇa,
The women in a family become corrupt;
And among fallen women, O Vārṣṇeya (Kṛṣṇa), caste-mixture arises.

42. This mixing brings both the family and its destroyers to hell,
For the spirits of their ancestors fall
When deprived of their offerings of rice and water.

43. By these evils of those who destroy a family
And create caste mixtures,
The immemorial *dharmas* of caste and family are destroyed.

44. We have heard, O Janārdana,
That a place in hell is reserved
For men of a family whose *dharmas* are destroyed.

45. Alas, we have resolved to commit a great sin
By undertaking to slay our own kin
Out of greed for the joys of kingship.

46. It would be better for me if Dhṛtarāṣṭra's sons,
Would slay me, weapons in hand,
Unarmed and unresisting, in battle.

47. Having spoken thus in the battle field,
Arjuna threw down his bow and arrow and sank down upon his chariot seat,
His mind overcome by grief.

This is the end of the first chapter, entitled "The Yoga of Arjuna's Crisis" *(arjunaviṣādayoga)*.

Chapter 2

THE YOGA OF UNDERSTANDING

Saṃjaya said:

1. To him who was thus burdened with sadness,
His eyes filled with tears and confused, who was sinking into depression,
Madhusūdana (Kṛṣṇa) spoke these words:

The Blessed One said:

2. Whence came to you this weakness in this (moment of) crisis?
It is ignoble, O Arjuna,
And neither leads to heaven nor brings glory.

3. Yield not to such unmanliness, Son of Pṛthā,
It does not befit you!
Having relinquished this petty faintheartedness, stand up, O Foe-Destroyer!

Arjuna said:

4. O Madhusūdana (Kṛṣṇa), how am I to fight with arrows
Against Bhīṣma and Droṇa,
Both worthy of reverence?

5. Surely it would be better to be even a beggar in this world
Than to have slain those mighty teachers.
For having slain them, wealth-desiring though they are,
I would enjoy only blood-smeared pleasures here on earth.

6. We know not which is better for us,
To conquer them or that they should conquer us.
For having slain those sons of Dhṛtarāṣṭra standing there before us,
We would not desire to live.

7. My inmost being is stricken by this flaw of pity,
For my mind is confused about *dharma,* I ask you which would be better?
Tell me decisively, I am your pupil;
Instruct me who have come to you.

8. For I do not myself see what would take from me this grief
Which dries up my senses,
Even if I gained sole rule over a thriving kingdom on earth,
Or even sovereignty over the gods.

Saṃjaya said:

9. Having so spoken to Hṛṣīkeśa (Kṛṣṇa),
And having said to Govinda, 'I will not fight!'
Guḍākeśa became silent.

10. Then, O Bhārata (Dhṛtarāṣṭra), Hṛṣīkeśa (Kṛṣṇa), as it were smiling,
Spoke these words to him who was sinking into depression
In the middle of the two armies:

The Blessed One said:

11. You grieve for those who are not to be grieved for,
Yet you speak words that sound like wisdom.
The wise do not grieve for the dead or for the living.

12. Never was there a time when I was not,
Nor you nor these rulers of men;
And never hereafter shall there be a time when any of us will not be.

13. For just as the embodied (one) comes to childhood, youth and old age in this body,
So he comes to another body (after departure from this body form):
The intelligent man is not deluded by this.

14. It is contact with objects of the senses, O Son of Kuntī (Arjuna),
That yield pleasure and pain, cold and heat,
These conditions are not lasting,
They come and go. Endure them, O Bhārata (Arjuna).

15. For he whom these do not disturb, O Bull among men,
The intelligent man who remains the same amidst pleasure and pain,
He is fit for immortality.

16. Of what-is-not there is no coming to be;
Of what-is there is no ceasing to be.
The final truth of these is also known to those who see the truth.

17. Know that that by which all this is pervaded, is indestructible;
Nothing can work the destruction of this which is imperishable.

18. These bodies, it is said, come to an end,
(But they belong) to an embodied one who is eternal, indestructible, immeasurable.
Therefore, fight, O Bhārata!

19. Both he who considers this to be slayer
And he who considers this to be slain,
Fail to understand: this neither slays nor is slain.

20. Nor is it ever born, nor dies,
Nor having come to be will it not be once again.
Unborn, eternal, everlasting,
This primeval one is not slain when the body is slain.

21. He who knows this which is indestructible, eternal, unborn, changeless,
How and whom does this man slay or cause another to slay, O Son of Pṛthā (Arjuna)?

22. Just as a man, casts off clothes and takes on new ones,
So the embodied one, casts off worn-out bodies
And takes on others that are new.

23. Weapons do not cut it, fire does not burn it,
Water does not wet it, winds do not dry it.

24. It is not able to be cleaved in two, burned, wetted, dried;
It is eternal, all-pervasive, unchanging, and immovable.

25. This is said to be unmanifest, unthinkable, invariable.
Therefore, knowing it as such, you should not grieve.

26. And likewise, even if you think this is perpetually born and perpetually dying,
Even so, O Strong-Armed, you should not grieve for this.

27. For to one born, death is certain,
And to one dying, birth is certain.
Therefore you must not grieve over what is unavoidable.

28. Beings are unmanifested in their beginnings, apparent in their middles,
And unmanifested in their ends:
What in this is to be lamented, O Bhārata?

29. Some take this for a marvel, others speak of this as a marvel,
And others hear of this as a marvel;
But even having heard of this, no one knows it yet.

30. This embodied one in the body of each, is eternal and invulnerable:
Therefore, O Bhārata, you must not grieve for any being!

31. Moreover, having regard to your own *dharma,* you must not falter.
There is no higher good for a *kṣatriya*
Than to fight accordant with *dharma.*

32. Happy is the *kṣatriya,* Son of Pṛthā,
Who meets with such a fight which, falling to his lot by chance,
Throws open the door of heaven.

33. But if you will not engage in this righteous battle,
Then having forsaken your own particular *dharma* as well as glory,
You will incur sin.

34. Besides, men will recount your unalterable dishonor;
And for one who has been held in honor,
Dishonor is worse than death.

35. Great warriors will think you withdrew from battle out of fear,
And you, having been highly thought of by them,
Will be made light of.

36. Your enemies will speak many unseemly words,
Scorning your courage.
What could be more painful than that?

37. Either, slain you will gain heaven,
Or victorious, you will enjoy the earth.
Therefore, stand up, Son of Kuntī, resolved to fight.

38. Treating pleasure and pain, gain and loss, victory and defeat as all alike,
Become readied for battle.
Thus you will not incur sin.

39. This (preceding) wisdom declared to you is the (wisdom of) *Sāṃkhya;*
But listen to the following wisdom of Yoga, O son of Pṛthā;
When disciplined with it, son of Pṛthā, you will leave behind the bondage of *karma.*

40. In this path, there is no unsuccessful effort,
No reversal is known;
Even a little of this *dharma* rescues one from great fear.

41. In this, O Joy-of-the-Kurus, understanding is resolute and unitary;
Many-branched, indeed, and endless is the understanding of him who is not resolute.

42. The undiscerning who delight in flowery words,
Who rejoice in the letter of the Veda, O son of Pṛthā,
Saying that there is nothing else,

43. Whose selves are made of desire, whose highest goal is heaven,
Who are full of ritual acts for the sake of enjoyment and power,
They only gather rebirth as the fruit of these actions *(karman)*.

44. The intellect of those men devoted to enjoyment and power,
Robbed of insight by these (words) is not established in meditation *(samādhi)*.

45. The Vedas deal with three *guṇas;* but you, Arjuna, become free of the three *guṇas*
Constantly take your stand in *sattva:* (light, wisdom)
Free of dualities, free of acquisition-and-possession, self-possessed.

46. For a *brāhman* who understands, (who knows what stands-under)
There is as much use in all the Vedas
As there is in a well when there is a flood of water on all sides.

47. Your interest is in action *(karman)* alone, never in its fruits:
Let not the fruit of action *(karman)* be what impels you,
But do not let yourself be attached to in-action *(akarman)* either.

48. Taking your stand in yoga, be active, O Winner of Wealth,
Having relinquished attachment and having gained equilibrium amidst success and failure.
Serenity of mind is called yoga.

49. Action *(karman)* is inferior by far indeed to the disciplined-intellect *(buddhiyoga),* O Winner of Wealth;

Seek refuge in *buddhi*.
Pitiful are those who are impelled by the fruit of action *(karman)*.

50. One whose intellect is disciplined leaves behind good and evil while on earth.
Therefore become readied for yoga,
For yoga is skill in action *(karman)*.

51. Having relinquished the fruit born of action *(karman)*,
Having disciplined their understanding,
The wise are free from the bondage of birth,
And arrive at a state which is beyond delusion.

52. When your intellect shall cross over the tangle of delusion,
Then you will become unattached
To what has been or will be heard (from the Veda).

53. When your intellect, turned this way and that from what you have heard (the Veda),
Shall stand in meditation *(samādhi)*, immovable,
Then you will attain yoga.

Arjuna said:
54. What is the mark of the man of firm wisdom,
Of the one who is centered in meditation *(samādhi)*, O Keśava?
How might the man of steady wisdom speak?
How might he walk, how sit?

The Blessed One said:
55. When a man forsakes all the desires of his mind, O Son of Pṛthā (Arjuna),
And through himself becomes content in his self alone,
Then, he is said to be of firm wisdom.

56. He whose mind is not troubled in the midst of sorrows,
Is free from desire in the midst of pleasures,
From whom passion, fear, and anger have departed,
He is said to be a sage of steady-wisdom.

57. He who has no attachment to anything,
And who neither rejoices nor is upset when he obtains good or evil,
His wisdom is firmly established.

58. When he, like a tortoise drawing in his limbs,
Withdraws his senses altogether from sense objects,
His wisdom is firmly established.

59. The objects of sense recede from the embodied one who abstains from feeding on them,
But a taste for such things persists.
Even that taste recedes, however, when the highest has been seen.

60. But, O Son of Kuntī, even the excited senses of a wise man
Endeavoring to make his way toward fulfillment,
Forcibly carry away his mind.

61. Having held all these in check, he should sit disciplined,
Intent on me; for he whose senses are submissive,
His intelligence is firmly established.

62. When a man dwells upon objects of sense,
Attachment to them is born.
From attachment, desire is born,
And from such desire anger arises.

63. From anger arises delusion, and from delusion loss of memory.
From loss of memory the destruction of intelligence,
And from this destruction, he perishes.

64. But that man finds clarity of mind,
Who moves among things of sense with his senses under control,
Free from desire and aversion
And who is thus self-controlled.

65. And in that clarity, the cessation of all his sorrows is born.
For the intelligence of a calm mind is quickly re-established.

66. For the one uncontrolled, there is no intelligence,
Nor is there realization;
And without realization there is no peace,
And how can there be happiness without peace?

67. Verily, the mind which yields to the roving senses,
Carries away man's understanding,
Like a wind carrying away a ship on the waters.

68. Therefore, O Mighty-Armed (Arjuna),
His intelligence is firmly established
Whose senses do not have sense-objects as an end.

69. When it is night for all beings, then the man of self-discipline is awake;
When beings are awake, then is night for the sage who sees.

70. He attains peace into whom all desires flow like waters entering the sea,
Though he is always being filled, he is always unaffected,
And not one who cherishes desires.

71. The man who abandons all desires, and acts without yearning,
Without possessiveness, without ego (not making himself to be the doer),
He finds peace.

72. O Son of Pṛthā, having reached this eternal state,
One does not again become bewildered and deluded.
Fixed in it up to the end of his time
He attains Brahman–Nirvāṇa.

This is the end of Chapter II, called "The Yoga of Understanding" *(sāṃkhyayoga)*.

Plate 2. Arjuna being driven in his chariot by Kṛṣṇa. (From *The Crīmadbhāgavatam*, Book I, by M. N. Chatterjee, published by Sasi Mohan Datta, Calcutta, 1895.)

Chapter 3

THE YOGA OF ACTION

Arjuna said:

1. If to your mind (the discipline of) understanding is superior to (the discipline of) action, O Janārdana,
Then why, O Keśava (Kṛṣṇa), do you enjoin me to the dreadful deed?

2. You are bewildering my understanding with these apparently confused propositions.
Therefore, tell me unequivocally
The one way by which I may gain what is good.

The Blessed One said:

3. Long ago, Blameless-One, I proclaimed a two-fold path of (living in) this world;
The path of knowledge *(jñānayoga)* for men of discrimination *(sāṃkhya)*
And the path of action *(karmayoga)* for men of action (yogins).

4. No man attains freedom from the bondage of action *(naiṣkarmya)*
Simply by not undertaking actions:
Nor by mere renunciation does one attain perfection.

5. For no one can remain absolutely inactive even for a moment.
Everyone is made to engage in action, however unwillingly,
By way of the *guṇas* born of *prakṛti.*

6. He who controls his powers of action, but continues to remember sense objects with his mind,
Is deluded and is to be called a hypocrite.

7. But he who controls his senses by his mind, O Arjuna,
And, without attachment, engages the action-senses in *karmayoga,*
He excels.

8. Do your allotted action,
For action is superior to inaction.
Even the maintenance of your body cannot be accomplished without action.

9. Except for the action engaged in as sacrifice,
This world is subject to the bondage of action.
For the sake of that, Son of Kuntī,
Perform action free from attachment as a sacrifice.

10. Long ago, Prajāpati created creatures together with sacrifice, and said:
By this shall you prosper,
Let this be the milch-cow for your desires.

11. By this, nourish the gods, and may the gods nourish you;
Thus nourishing each other, you will attain to the supreme good.

12. For the gods, nourished by the sacrifice,
Will give you the enjoyments you desire.
He who enjoys their gifts without giving to them in return,
Is nothing but a thief.

13. Good men, eating of the remains of the sacrifice,
Are free from all sins,
But wicked men who prepare food for their own sake alone (not sharing with the gods and others),
Eat sin.

14. Beings arise from food;
Food is produced from rain;
Rain arises from the sacrifice,
And sacrifice is born of action.

15. Know that action has its origin in Brahman (the Veda),
And the Brahman has its origin in the imperishable.
Therefore, Brahman, the all-pervading,
Is always grounded in sacrifice.

16. He who on earth does not contribute
To the continued movement of the wheel thus set in motion, is evil, O Son of Pṛthā;
Delighting in the senses, he lives in vain.

17. The man, however, who can be delighted in his self alone,
Who is pleased with the self and content only with the self,
For him there is no work to be done.

18. He has no interest in this world
To gain by what is done or by what is not done.
He is not dependent on any of these beings for any advantage.

19. Therefore, perform the action that has to be done,
Continually free from attachment,
For by performing action without attachment,
A man reaches the supreme.

20. For by action alone, it was,
That Janaka and others ascended to perfection.
And also you must act,
Attending to no less than the holding together of the world.

21. For whatever the superior man does,
That other people also do.
He sets the standard which the world follows.

22. For me, O Son of Pṛthā,
There is no work whatever to be done in the three worlds,
Nothing unobtained which is to be obtained;
Yet without fail, I continue in action.

23. For if I were not ever unweariedly engaged in action,
Son of Pṛthā,
Men everywhere would follow my path.

24. These worlds would be destroyed if I did not perform
action
And I would be the author of confusion,
And would destroy these people.

25. As those who are ignorant *(avidyā)* act from attachment
to action;
The wise should also act, O Bhārata,
But without attachment,
Desiring to act so as to hold the world together.

26. Let no wise man shake the minds of the ignorant who
are attached to action;
Acting with yoga-wisdom, let the wise make all action
attractive.

27. Actions are engaged in by way of the *guṇas* of *prakṛti*
alone;
Yet he who is deluded by the sense of I thinks "I am the
doer."

28. But O Strong-Armed, he who knows the truth
About the differentiation from *guṇas* and action, thinks
(and knows that):
Guṇas act upon *guṇas,*
He is not attached.

29. Those who are deluded by the *guṇas* of *prakṛti*
Are attached to the workings of the *guṇas.*
But let not him who knows the whole,
Unsettle the sluggish, who know only a part.

30. With your mind on the supreme self,
Surrendering all action to me,
And being free of desire and selfishness,
Your (mental) fever vanished, fight.

31. Men who constantly follow out this teaching of mine,
Uncomplaining and full of faith,
They too are released from (the bondage of) their actions.

32. But those who murmur against my teaching,
Who do not follow it out,
Know those mindless ones, deluded in all understanding,
To be lost.

33. Even the wise man functions in conformity with *prakṛti.*
Beings follow *prakṛti,*
What will suppression accomplish?

34. Attraction and repulsion for the objects of sense
Are seated in the senses.
Let no one come under the control of these two;
They are his worse enemies.

35. One's own *dharma,* even when not done perfectly,
Is better than someone else's *dharma,* even though well performed;
Indeed, death in one's own *dharma* is better,
For another's is perilous.

Arjuna said:
36. Then what, O Descendant of Vṛṣṇi,
Is that by which a man who performs evil, is bidden,
Even against his will,
Impelled so-to-speak by force?

The Blessed One said:
37. Desire it is, anger it is,
Produced from the *guṇa* of passion *(rajas),*
All-consuming and greatly sinful.
Know this to be the enemy here.

38. For just as fire is concealed by smoke,
A mirror by dust, and an embryo by the womb,
So is this (knowledge) concealed by that (passion).

39. Knowledge, O Son of Kuntī,
Is concealed by that constant enemy of the wise,
That insatiable flame of desire.

40. The senses, the mind *(manas),* the *buddhi,*
Are said to be its seat.
Having concealed knowledge through these,
It deludes the embodied one.

41. Therefore, having controlled the senses to begin with, O Best of the Bhāratas,
Slay this evil which brings loss of knowledge and understanding.

42. The senses are great, they say;
But the mind is above the senses, and *buddhi* above mind.
And above *buddhi* is He.

43. Thus having become aware of that which is greater than *buddhi,*
Having strengthened yourself through yourself,
Slay the enemy, Strong-Armed, which is so hard to get at,
And has the form of desire.

This is the third chapter, entitled "The Yoga of Action" *(karmayoga).*

Chapter 4

THE YOGA OF KNOWLEDGE

The Blessed One said:

1. I proclaimed this imperishable discipline (yoga) to Vivasvān,
He told it to Manu, and he, to Ikṣvāku.

2. Handed down in this way from one to another,
This yoga was known by the sage-kings,
But, Foe-Destroyer, it became lost on earth with the lapse of time.

3. This very yoga of old
Is being proclaimed by me to you today.
For you are devoted to me, and my friend,
And this yoga is, indeed, the supreme secret.

Arjuna said:

4. Later was your birth, earlier was the birth of Vivasvān:
How am I to understand this,
That you proclaimed this discipline (to him) in the beginning?

The Blessed One said:

5. Many are my past lives and yours, Arjuna;
I know them all, you do not, Foe-Destroyer.

6. Though I am unborn and of changeless self,
Though I am Lord of beings, having taken my stand over my own *prakṛti*
I am born by my own self's power *(māyā)*.

7. For whenever there is a decrease in *dharma,* O Bhārata,
And a rise in *adharma,*
Then I send forth myself.

8. For the protection of the good and the destruction of evil,
For the purpose of the establishment of *dharma,*
I am born from age to age.

9. He who knows in truth this, my divine birth and actions,
Having relinquished his body,
He goes not to rebirth but to me, Arjuna.

10. With passion, fear, and anger gone,
Taking refuge in me,
Being filled with me,
Many, purified by the exercise of wisdom,
Attain my state *(bhāva).*

11. In whatever way men approach me,
In the same way they receive their reward;
Men follow my path in every case, Son of Pṛthā.

12. Those desiring fulfillment of their actions on earth,
Sacrifice to the gods.
Quickly, indeed, comes fulfillment in the world of men from such actions.

13. I created the four classes by the differentiation of *guṇa* and *karma.*
Although I made them,
Know me as the imperishable non-doer.

14. Actions do not pollute me,
I do not covet their fruit.
He who knows me thus, is not bound by actions.

15. So knowing, the ancients who desired release were active.
You be active, therefore,
Just as the ancients were long ago.

16. What is action? What is inaction?
Even the wise are confused on this point.

I will declare to you that action which, if you know it,
You will be released from evil.

17. You must understand not only action, however,
But improper action *(vikarman)* and inaction *(akarman):*
The way of action is difficult to fathom.

18. He who can see action in inaction,
And inaction in action,
Is a wise man;
He does action in a disciplined way.

19. He whose every undertaking is free of compulsive desire,
Whose actions are burned up by the fire of knowledge,
Him the wise call learned.

20. Having relinquished attachment to the fruit of action,
(karmaphalāsaṇgaṃ, literally, "identification with the fruit of action")
Being constantly satisfied and without dependence.
He does nothing whatever,
Even though he is engaged in action.

21. Without craving, with mind restrained and relinquishing all possessions,
Being active with body alone,
He does not incur sin.

22. Content with what he happens to find,
Himself beyond the dualities, free from envy,
And the same in success and failure,
He is not bound even though he is acting.

23. The action of the unattached man is free,
Whose understanding is firmly rooted in knowledge,
And who acts as a sacrifice, is wholly dissolved.

24. The act of offering is Brahman, the oblation (offered) is Brahman,
It is poured by Brahman in the fire of Brahman.
Brahman becomes he whose actions are centered on Brahman.

25. Some yogins offer sacrifice to the gods only,
While others make sacrifice by sacrificing the sacrifice itself.

26. There are others who offer hearing and their other senses
Into the fires of equanimity;
Others sacrifice sense objects, into the fire of the senses.

27. Others offer up all the actions of all the senses
And of the vital-breath
Into the fire of the disciplined concentration (yoga) of self-restraint
Which is kindled by knowledge.

28. Others offer as sacrifice their possessions, their austerity,
Or their yogic exercises;
While still others of firmly restrained minds and austere vows,
Offer their scriptural study (Veda) and their knowledge (of it).

29. Others, likewise, having controlled the course of their inbreathing and outbreathing *(prāṇāpānagatī ruddhvā),*
Wholly devoted to breath control *(praṇāyāmaparāyaṇāḥ)*
Sacrifice the one breath into the other *(apāne juhvati prāṇaṃ).*

30. And others, the abstemious in food,
Offer as sacrifice their life breaths in life breaths.
All these are knowers of sacrifice,
And by sacrifice their sins are destroyed.

31. Those who eat the food of immortality left after the sacrifice,
Attain the primeval Brahman.
Not even this world is for one who does not sacrifice,
How then the next world, Highest of the Kurus?

32. Thus manifold sacrifices are spread out in the face of Brahman.

Know them all to be born of action.
Knowing this, you will be freed.

33. The sacrifice of knowledge is better, Foe–Destroyer,
Than the sacrifice of material things.
All action without exception is completely terminated in knowledge, O Son of Pṛthā.

34. Know this by obeisance, by inquiry, and by service to them.
Men of wisdom, the seers of truth,
Will explain to you this knowledge.

35. You will never be deluded again, Son of Pāṇḍu,
When you have learned this:
For by this you will see all beings without exception in yourself and in me.

36. Even if you were among sinners the worse of sinners,
You will cross beyond all evil
By the boat of knowledge alone.

37. Just as a kindled fire reduces its fuel to ashes, Arjuna,
So the fire of knowledge reduces all action to ashes.

38. For no equal to wisdom as a purifier is known on earth.
This, the one reaching his own ultimate fulfillment in yoga
Finds in himself with time.

39. He who has faith, who is committed to it, whose senses are controlled,
Gains knowledge, and having obtained it,
He quickly attains supreme peace.

40. But he who is without insight and is without faith,
His very self being doubt,
He is lost:
For the doubting one, there is neither this world nor the next,
Nor is there happiness.

41. Actions do not blind him, O Wealth-Winner,
Who has renounced all actions in yoga,
Who has cut out doubt by knowledge,
And who is self-possessed.

42. Therefore, having cut out with your self's own sword of knowledge,
This doubt in your heart which is born of ignorance,
Get into yoga and raise yourself up, O Bhārata.

This is the fourth chapter, entitled "The Yoga of Knowledge" *(jñānayoga)*.

Chapter 5

THE YOGA OF RENUNCIATION OF ACTION

Arjuna said:

1. Kṛṣṇa, you praise the renunciation of actions,
And then again, their disciplined undertaking.
Which one of these is the better one:
Tell me quite decisively.

The Blessed One said:

2. The renunciation and the yoga of action
Both bring the ultimate good,
But of the two, the yoga of action is better than the renunciation of action.

3. He who neither hates nor desires,
Is to be known as one who constantly renounces.
For free from dualities, O Strong-Armed,
He is easily released from bondage.

4. It is the childish, not the men of learning,
Who declare *Sāṃkhya* and Yoga to be diverse.
He who takes his stand in either one properly,
Obtains the fruit of both.

5. That place and standing which is attained by (the men of) *Sāṃkhya,*
Is reached also by Yoga.
Sāṃkhya and Yoga are one:
He who sees this sees truly.

6. Renunciation, O Strong-Armed, is difficult to attain without yoga.
The sage who is disciplined in yoga
Attains to Brahman quickly.

7. Committed to yoga, himself pure in mind,
His senses conquered, his self conquered
And his self having become the self of all beings,
He is not polluted even when he acts.

8. "I am doing nothing at all."
So the disciplined one who knows the truth thinks:
Seeing, hearing, touching, smelling, tasting,
Walking, sleeping, breathing,

9. Talking, grasping and letting go,
Opening and closing his eyes,
He keeps present that in these, only the senses are active among sense-objects.

10. Having placed his actions in Brahman,
Having relinquished attachment,
One who acts is not touched by sin,
Just as the lotus leaf is not wet by water.

11. For self-purification, men of disciplined effort (yogins)
Are active only by way of the body, mind, understanding or the senses,
Without attachment.

12. The disciplined man, having relinquished the fruit of action,
Attains perfect peace.
The undisciplined man, impelled by desire,
Is attached to the fruit and is bound.

13. Having renounced with his mind all actions,
The embodied one sits at ease,
In the city of nine gates (the body),
Neither acting nor causing action.

14. That one stands over what is born,
Neither creates agency of the world, nor actions, nor the

conjunction of action with the fruit
Rather, this is a natural power *(svabhāvaḥ).*

15. This pervasive one does not take on anyone's sin
Nor his good deeds either.
Knowledge is concealed by ignorance:
With this, creatures are deluded.

16. But for those in whom ignorance is destroyed by knowledge,
For them knowledge brightens the highest (in them) like the sun.

17. Fixed on that (highest vision), the self open to that,
With commitment to that,
They attain a condition from where there is no return;
Their sins removed by knowledge.

18. Men of learning view with equal eye a Brahman of knowledge and good learning,
A cow, an elephant, and even a dog and an outcaste.

19. Creation is overcome, even here on earth,
By those whose minds are established in equality.
For Brahman is the same, without defect to all.
Therefore they are firm and abiding in Brahman.

20. One should not exult on gaining the pleasant,
Nor should one be dismayed on meeting the unpleasant.
His understanding steady, undeluded,
The knower of Brahman is centered on Brahman.

21. The self which is unattached to external contacts
Finds happiness in himself.
Being joined by yoga to Brahman
He obtains undecaying happiness.

22. For those pleasures which are born of contact
Are merely sources of sorrow, possessing a beginning and an end.
The man who is awake takes no delight in them, O Son of Kuntī.

23. The man who here on earth, before giving up his body,
Is able to hold out against the force born of desire and anger,
He is disciplined, he is happy.

24. He who is happy within, whose joy is within,
And whose light is within,
He becomes Brahman and goes on to the happiness of Brahman.

25. Those sages whose sins are destroyed,
Whose indecisions are dispelled, whose selves are disciplined,
And who rejoice in the welfare of every being,
Attain to the happiness of Brahman.

26. To those wise men who have destroyed desire and anger,
Who have controlled their minds, and realized the self,
The happiness of Brahman is near.

27. Having shut out external contacts
And fixed the eye in the middle between the two brows,
Having equalized the two breaths moving within the nostrils,

28. Having controlled the senses, mind and intelligence,
The sage who has freedom as his goal,
Who has cast away desire, fear and anger,
Is freed forever.

29. Knowing me as the enjoyer of sacrifices and austerities,
As the great lord of all the worlds,
A friend of all beings,
One attains peace.

This is the fifth chapter, entitled "The Yoga of Renunciation of Action" *(karmasaṃnyāsayoga)*.

Chapter 6

THE YOGA OF MEDITATION

The Blessed One said:

1. He who does the action that has to be done
But without resting on its fruit,
Is a man of disciplined engagement in action,
He is a yogin, a man of renunciation,
And not he who is without sacrificial fire and without ritual actions.

2. What is called renunciation,
Know it to be the disciplined engagement in action, O Son of Pāṇḍu.
For no one becomes a yogin
Who has not renounced compulsive purpose.

3. Action is the medium for the sage who desires to ascend to yoga;
Tranquillity is the medium of him who has already ascended to such yoga.

4. For when one has renounced all compulsive purpose and
Is attached neither to actions nor to sense-objects,
He is then said to have ascended to yoga.

5. Let a man lift his self by his own self;
Let him not lower himself;
One's self alone is one's own self's friend and foe.

6. One's self is friend of one's self when self-conquered;
But the self of one not so self-possessed,
Becomes hostile like an enemy.

7. The higher self of one who is self-conquered and at peace,
Is composed amidst cold and heat, pleasure and pain, honor and dishonor.

8. The yogin who is satisfied with wisdom and understanding,
Who is unshaken, with his senses conquered,
To whom gold, a stone, a clod of earth are the same,
Is said to be disciplined.

9. He excels whose understanding is the same,
Amidst the well-disposed, the friendly, the neutral arbiter and hostile,
Amidst enemies and allies,
Amidst the righteous and the sinful.

10. Let the yogin always concentrate his mind,
Living alone in solitude, his mind and self restrained,
Without cravings and (longing for) possessions.

11. Let him fix for himself on a clean place a firm seat,
Which is neither too high nor too low,
Made of Kuśa grass, a deerskin, and a cloth,
One over the other.

12. Sitting on that seat, making his mind one-pointed,
Controlling the activity of his mind and senses,
Let him engage in yoga for the purification of the self.

13. Let him hold his body, neck, and head erect and motionless,
Looking fixedly at the tip of his nose,
Not looking in any direction.

14. And having his thoughts on me, absorbed in me,
With the self calm and free from fear
And keeping his vow of celibacy,
Let him sit disciplined.

15. Thus continually disciplining himself and with his mind controlled,

He attains peace, the supreme bliss,
That which exists in me.

16. Yoga is not for one who eats too much or not at all.
It is not for him, Arjuna, who sleeps too much or too little.

17. For one whose enjoyment of food and pleasure is disciplined,
Whose engagement in actions is disciplined,
Whose sleeping and waking are disciplined,
Yoga becomes a destroyer of sorrow.

18. When one's controlled mind abides in one's self alone,
Freed from yearning,
Then one is said to be disciplined.

19. Unflickering, like a lamp in a sheltered place:
So the man of disciplined thought
Practicing yoga of the self.

20. That in which thought ceases,
Stopped by the practice of disciplined concentration,
And in which, seeing himself through himself,
One is content in himself;

21. That in which he knows that which is boundless happiness,
Beyond the senses but perceivable by understanding,
And in which, established,
He knows this and swerves not from the truth;

22. That which, having obtained it,
One thinks there is no further gain beyond it,
And in which he is established,
By no sorrow, however heavy, is he shaken;

23. Let this disengagement of the connection with sorrow
Be known as yoga.
This yoga is to be practiced with determination,
With a mind free from depression.

24. Abandoning entirely all desires originating in compulsive purpose,
Having exercised restraint on every side
Over all the senses by the mind,

25. Let him be stilled little by little,
Through understanding firmly grounded;
And fixing his mind on the self,
Let him not set his thoughts on anything else.

26. Having restrained the mind, restless, unsteady,
From whatever it goes out to,
Let him bring it into the control of his self alone.

27. Indeed, the highest happiness comes to the yogin
Whose mind is peaceful,
In whom passions are at rest, who is sinless, has become Brahman.

28. Continually exercising himself in disciplined-concentration in this way,
The yogin free from his sin,
Easily attains to the boundless happiness in touch with Brahman.

29. The one whose self is disciplined by yoga,
Sees the self abiding in every being
And sees every being in the self;
He sees the same in all beings.

30. He who sees me everywhere, and sees all in me,
I am not lost to him, and he is not lost to me.

31. He who standing in oneness,
Worships me abiding in all beings,
Exists in me, whatever happens.

32. When one sees the pleasure or pain of others
To be equal to one's own, O Arjuna,
He is considered the highest yogin.

Arjuna said:
33. You have proclaimed yoga of sameness, O Madhusūdana,

But I do not see a firm grounding of this yoga
Because of man's restlessness.

34. Restless, indeed, is the mind, O Kṛṣṇa,
It is turbulent, strong and hard.
Its restraint, I think, would be as difficult to accomplish as controlling the wind.

The Blessed One said:

35. Doubtless, Strong-Armed, the mind is restless and hard to restrain,
But by practice and nonattachment,
It can be held, Son of Kuntī.

36. Yoga is impossible to attain with an unrestrained self:
So I think.
But it can be attained with a controlled self
In skillful ways.

Arjuna said:

37. What way does one go, O Kṛṣṇa,
Who is undisciplined but possesses faith,
And whose mind swerves away from yoga
Before he has obtained the ultimate fulfillment in yoga?

38. Fallen from both, not having become firm,
And bewildered over the path to Brahman,
Does he not perish, O Strong-Armed,
Like a severed rain cloud?

39. You must cut off completely this doubt of mine, O Kṛṣṇa,
For there is no remover of this doubt
Other than you to be found.

The Blessed One said:

40. Son of Pṛthā, neither in this world nor the next does such a one know destruction.
For, my dear one, no one who does good goes to an evil end.

41. Having attained the worlds of the meritorious,
Having dwelled there many years,
The one who has fallen from yoga
Is born in a house of the pure and prosperous.

42. Or else he is born in a family of wise yogins:
Of course, such a birth in the world is more difficult to obtain.

43. There, he gains the mental traits of his previous embodiment,
And once more from that point
He strives for fulfillment, O Joy of the Kurus.

44. By his previous practise alone,
He is carried onward,
Even without willing this.
He who desires the knowledge of yoga is beyond the Vedic rule.

45. But the yogin who strives with perseverence,
Who is purified of sin,
And is perfected through many lives
Goes to the highest goal.

46. The yogin is greater than the ascetic,
He is considered greater than the men of knowledge;
He is greater than doers of ritual works:
Therefore, become a yogin, O Arjuna.

47. Of all yogins, the one who full of faith,
Worships me with his inner self given over to me,
I consider him to be nearest to my vision.

This ends the sixth chapter, entitled "The Yoga of Meditation" *(dhyānayoga)*

Chapter 7

THE YOGA OF WISDOM AND UNDERSTANDING

The Blessed One said:

1. Hear this, O Son of Pṛthā, by fastening your mind on me,
By practicing yoga, relying on me,
You will gain knowledge of me fully, without doubt.

2. I will tell you the whole of this wisdom
Accompanied by knowledge which, when known,
There remains nothing more on earth to be known.

3. Scarcely one man in thousands strives for perfection,
And of those who strive and are successful,
Perhaps one knows me in essence.

4. Earth, water, fire, air, ether, mind, understanding, and the sense of I:
This is my *prakṛti* which is divided eight-fold.

5. This is my lower *prakṛti.*
But know now, O Strong-Armed, my other *prakṛti,*
Supreme and the source of life,
By which the world is supported.

6. Know that all beings have this for their womb.
I am the origin of the world
And also its dissolution.

7. There is nothing whatever above me, O Wealth-Winner.
All this (world) is strung on me
Like jewels on a string.

8. I am the taste in the waters, O Son of Kuntī,
I am the radiance in the sun and moon;
The sacred syllable *(Oṃ)* in all the Vedas,
The sound in ether, and manliness in men.

9. I am the pleasant fragrance in earth,
The glowing brightness in fire,
The life in all beings,
The austerity in ascetics.

10. Know me to be the seed of all beings, O Son of Pṛthā.
I am the understanding of the wise,
The splendor of the splendid.

11. I am the strength of the strong, O Master of the Bhāratas,
Devoid of desire and passion.
I am that desire in all beings which is not incompatible with *dharma*.

12. And know also that whatever conditions (in beings) are *sattvic* (lucid) *rajasic* (active) or even *tamasic* (indolent),
Are from me alone.
But I am not in them,
They are in me.

13. Deluded by these conditions composed of the three *guṇas*,
This whole world does not recognize me,
Changeless and above them.

14. For this divine *māyā* (elusive power) of mine composed of the *guṇas*,
Is difficult to transcend.
Only those who resort to me,
Cross beyond this deluding power *(māyā)*.

15. Foolish evil-doers, lowest of men,
Whose understanding is carried away by this deluding power *(māyā)*
And whose essence is bound (to their actions),
Do not resort to me.

16. Men of good deeds who worship me, O Arjuna,
Are of four kinds:
The afflicted, the seekers of knowledge, the seeker of wealth,
And also, O Bull of the Bhāratas, the wise.

17 Of these, the wise, always whole,
And whose committment is to the One, excels.
Indeed, I am exceedingly dear to the wise,
And he is dear to me.

18. Noble are all these without exception,
But to my mind, the wise is my very self.
For he with disciplined self-effort *(yuktātmā)*
Is firmly grounded in me alone as the highest goal.

19. At the end of many births,
The man of wisdom comes to me
Aware that Vāsudeva is all.
Such a man of great self is very hard to find.

20. Those whose understanding has been carried away by one desire or another,
Flee to other gods,
Having carried out one or another observance,
Led by their own (bound) *prakṛti.*

21. I make unshakeable the faith of any devotee
Who wishes to worship with faith any form whatever.

22. Disciplined with that faith,
He seeks the propitiation of such a manifestation (god),
And from it he gains his desires.
Indeed, it is I who ordains (the benefits) of those desires.

23. But transient is that fruit of those of little intelligence.
Those who sacrifice to the gods, go to the gods;
But those who are dedicated to me, go to me.

24. Those without understanding think me, the nonapparent,
To have appeared,
Not being cognizant of my supreme nature, changeless and unsurpassed.

25. Covered by my elusive power *(yoga-māyā),*
I do not appear to all.
The world is deluded and does not recognize me, unborn, imperishable.

26. I know the beings of the past, present and yet to be, O Arjuna,
But no one verily knows me.

27. All beings at birth are subject to delusion, O Descendant of Bhārata,
By the illusion arising from the pairs of opposites,
Desire and aversion, O Conqueror of the Foe.

28. But those men of meritorious deeds in whom sin has come to an end,
Who are thus released from the illusion of opposites,
Worship me, steadfast in their resolutions
(dṛdhavratāḥ).

29. Having taken refuge in me,
Those who strive *(yatanti)* for release from death and old age
Know Brahman entirely and the self and all action.

30. Those who with disciplined minds know me in my higher and lower domains
And the physical world and the highest sacrifice,
Know me even at the time of death.

This is the seventh chapter, entitled "The Yoga of Wisdom and Understanding" *(jñānavijñānayoga).*

Chapter 8

THE YOGA OF THE IMPERISHABLE BRAHMAN

Arjuna said:

1. What is that Brahman? What is the original self?
What is action *(karma),* O Best of Men?
What is said to be the higher and what the lower domain?

2. How and what is the sacrifice here in this body, O Slayer of Madhu?
And how are you to be cognized by those of disciplined self
At the time of death?

The Blessed One said:

3. The imperishable is Brahman, the supreme;
The higher self is called its very essence *(svabhāvah):*
And *karman* is the creative force that causes creatures to exist.

4. A perishable condition is the basis of the lower domain;
The *puruṣa* (vision) is the basis of the higher domain;
I am the ground of all sacrifice here in the body, O best of the embodied ones.

5. And at the time of death,
Whoever, leaving the body remembers me alone,
He attains my being: of this there is no doubt.

6. Whatever is in his mind at the time of death, O Son of Kuntī,
Only that he becomes; embodied in that state.

7. Therefore, think on me at all times and fight;
With mind and understanding joined to me,
Without doubt you will come to me alone.

8. He who is disciplined by the effort of yoga, not wandering elsewhere,
And concentrates on the supreme shining vision *(puruṣa),*
He goes to him, O Son of Pṛthā.

9. He who meditates on the ancient seer, the ruler,
Who is more minute than minute, the supporter of all,
Incomprehensible in form, sun-colored and beyond darkness:

10. He, engaged in devotion with an immovable mind
And having succeeded by virtue of this disciplined effort (yoga)
In making his life-breath go to the mid-point between his eyebrows,
He, at the time of death, attains shining fullness of vision *(puruṣa).*

11. That which the Veda-knowers designate as the imperishable,
Which the restrained ones free of passion enter,
And desiring which they undertake a life of chastity:
That abode, I will declare to you briefly.

12. He who controls all the gates of the body
And confines the mind to the heart,
Has set his breath in the head
And established himself in concentration by yoga,

13. He who utters *Oṃ,* which is Brahman,
Meditates on me as he goes forth and abandons his body,
He reaches the highest goal.

14. He whose thought is never on anything but me,
Who constantly remembers me:
For that man of disciplined effort ever disciplined,
I am easily reached, O Son of Pṛthā.

15. Having come to me,
Those men of great self do not go to rebirth
The place of pain and impermanence,
But have reached the supreme fullness.

16. The worlds from the realm of Brahmā down,
Are subject to rebirth, O Arjuna;
But having come to me, O Son of Kuntī,
There is no rebirth.

17. The men who know the day of Brahmā, long as a thousand ages,
And the night of Brahmā, equally as long,
Are knowers of what day and night are.

18. All apparent things arise from the non-apparent at the coming of day,
And at the coming of night they are dissolved there,
In this so-called nonapparent.

19. This very same multitude of beings,
Coming forth repeatedly,
Dissolve helplessly at the coming of night, O Son of Pṛthā,
And arises at the coming of day.

20. Higher than this nonapparent state is another nonapparent state,
Which does not perish even with the perishing of all beings.

21. It is called the imperishable, and the supreme destination,
Those who reach it do not return.
This is my supreme dwelling place.

22. This is the fullness of vision,
By whom all this is pervaded,
In whom all beings stand.
It is to be gained by unswerving dedication.

23. O Best of the Bhāratas, I will declare that time at which men of discipline,
Depart, go and do not return,
And when they depart, but do return.

24. Fire, light, day, the bright half of the lunar cycle,
The six months of the sun's northerly course:
Departing then, men who are knowers of Brahman
Go to Brahman.

25. Smoke, night, the dark half of the lunar period,
The six months of the sun's southerly course:
Departing then, the man of discipline
Reaches the light of the moon and returns.

26. These bright and dark paths of the world
Are thought to be everlasting:
By one, man goes and does not return,
By the other, man returns.

27. The man of discipline who knows these paths, O Son of Pṛthā,
Is not deluded.
Therefore, at all times be engaged in disciplined effort, O Arjuna.

28. The yogin who knows all this,
Transcends the fruit of deeds assigned in the Veda,
In sacrifices, austerities and alms-giving,
And goes to the supreme and primal place.

This is the eighth chapter, entitled "The Yoga of the Imperishable Brahman" *(akṣarabrahmayoga)*.

Chapter 9

THE YOGA OF SOVEREIGN KNOWLEDGE AND SOVEREIGN SECRET

The Blessed One said:

1. To you, however, who are uncomplaining,
I will declare this most secret wisdom joined with knowledge;
Knowing which, you will be released from evil.

2. This is sovereign knowledge, sovereign secret,
This utmost purifier is directly perceived,
Accordant with *dharma,* and quite easy to follow and imperishable.

3. Men who put no faith in this practice, O Foe–Destroyer,
Return to the path of wandering death and rebirth,
Not having reached me.

4. This whole world is pervaded by me in my unmanifested form.
Though all beings are *fixed* in me, I am not *fixed* in them.

5. Yet beings do not stand in me.
Behold my lordly secret:
Generating beings, yet not being generated by them,
My very self is the source of beings.

6. Know that just as the mighty wind, blowing everywhere,
Stands constantly in space,
So all beings stand in me.

7. All beings, O Son of Kuntī, go into my lower *prakṛti* at the time of a world cycle,
And I send them forth again at the beginning of a new cycle.

8. Having seized my own lower *prakṛti,*
I send forth this whole multitude of helpless beings again and again,
At the behest of my lower *prakṛti.*

9. And these actions, O Wealth-Winner, do not bind me,
Who remain as if indifferent,
Unattached to these actions.

10. Under my supervision, *prakṛti* brings forth the moving and the unmoving;
By this cause, O Son of Kuntī, the world revolves.

11. Deluded men, not aware of my supreme condition as Great Lord of Beings,
Despise me when taking a human form.

12. Fallen subject to the delusive *prakṛti*
Which is fiendish and binding *(āsurīm),*
They are mindless,
Their knowledge and deeds and hopes are vain.

13. But those of great self, who abide in my higher *prakṛti*
And who have a mind for no other and worship me, O Son of Pṛthā,
Knowing me as the imperishable source of all beings,

14. Ever celebrating me and striving with firm resolution,
And honoring me with devotion,
Attend upon me constantly ever disciplined.

15. And others also, sacrificing with the sacrifice of wisdom,
Attend upon me as the one, the distinct and as the many
Facing in all directions.

16. I am the ritual, the sacrifice, the oblation, the medicinal herb,
The Vedic text, the clarified butter, the fire and the offering.

17. I am the father of this world,
The mother, the supporter, the grandsire;
I am the one to be known, the purifier,
The sacred syllable *Oṃ,* the *Ṛk,* the *Sāma* and the *Yajus* (the verse, chant and sacrificial formula).

18. I am the witness, the presiding one, the bearer, the final shelter, abode, and friend;
I am the origin and dissolution and foundation:
I am the treasure house and imperishable seed.

19. I give heat, I give and withhold rain;
I am immortality as well as death,
Existence *(sat)* as well as nonexistence *(asat),* O Arjuna.

20. Knowers of the three (Vedas),
Having drunk the soma and become purified of sin,
Worship me with sacrifices and pray for the way to heaven.
Having reached the fair world of Indra,
They enjoy the pleasures of the gods in heaven.

21. Having enjoyed that spacious world of heaven,
Their merit exhausted, they enter the world of mortals.
Thus conforming to the practice enjoined in the three Vedas,
Cherishing desires, they gain what is transient.

22. Of the men who dedicate themselves to me, thinking on me alone,
And who are constant in their effort,
I bring acquisition and possession of their goal.

23. Even those who, devoted to other gods, sacrifice filled with faith,
Even they sacrifice to me alone, O Son of Kuntī,
Though not according to prescribed rules.

24. For I am the enjoyer of all sacrifices, and lord of all sacrifices,
But they do not perceive me in truth,
Hence, they fall.

25. Those who are avowed to the gods, go to the gods;
Those who are avowed to the ancestors, go to the ancestors;
Those who sacrifice to spirits, go to the spirits.
But those who sacrifice to me, come to me.

26. He who offers me with devotion a leaf, a flower, a fruit, water,
I accept that devotional offering of a pure self.

27. Make your doing, eating, sacrificing, giving, and undergoing austerity,
An offering to me, O Son of Kuntī.

28. Thus you will be freed from good and evil fruits,
Released from the bondage of action;
And with your self disciplined by the yoga of renunciation,
Released, you will come to me.

29. I am like-minded to all beings,
None is hateful or dear to me.
But those who worship me with devotion
Are in me, and I am in them also.

30. If a man of very evil conduct worships me in undivided devotion,
He too is to be thought righteous.
For he has decided rightly.

31. Swiftly he becomes one whose self is *dharma,*
And obtains everlasting peace.
Recognize, O Son of Kuntī, that no one dedicated to me perishes.

32. For having taken refuge in me, O Son of Pṛthā,
Even those who are born of sinful wombs, women, Vaiśyās and even Śūdras,
They also reach the highest goal.

33. How much more, then, meritorious brāhmans and devoted sage-kings.
Having entered this unhappy and perishable world, worship me.

34. Your mind fixed on me, be devoted to me;
Sacrificing to me, pay reverence to me;
Having thus a disciplined self and having me as final end,
You will come to me.

This is the ninth chapter, entitled "The Yoga of Sovereign Knowledge and Sovereign Secret" *(rājavidyārāja-guhyayoga)*.

Plate 3. Kṛṣṇa. (From *The The Crīmadbhāgavatam*, Book I, by M. N. Chatterjee, published by Sasi Mohan Datta, Calcutta, 1895.)

Chapter 10

THE YOGA OF MANIFESTATION

The Blessed One said:

1. Listen still further to my supreme word, O Strong-Armed,
Which out of desire for your welfare
I will declare to you who are taking delight in it.

2. Neither the multitude of gods nor the great sages know my origin,
For I am the source in every respect of gods and of great sages.

3. He who knows me, the unborn, the Great Lord of the World, without beginning,
He is undeluded among mortals and is released from all sins.

4. Understanding, wisdom, freedom from delusion,
Forbearance, truthfulness, self-control, tranquility;
Happiness, sorrow, existence, nonexistence, fear and lack of fear,

5. Non-violence, equanimity, contentment, austerity,
Generosity, fame and ill-fame,
These are the conditions of beings which arise from me alone.

6. The seven great sages of old, and likewise the four Manus,
Had their being from me, being born of my mind;
From them, are these creatures in the world.

7. He who knows in truth this expansiveness and yoga of mine,
Is enjoined by unfaltering yoga;
Of this, there is no doubt.

8. I am the origin of all; from me all proceeds;
Knowing this, the wise, adorned with creation, worship me.

9. Mindful of me, their lives centered on me,
Bringing each other to understand me
And constantly conversing about me,
They are content and rejoice in me.

10. To those so disciplined who worship me with love,
I give that yoga of understanding
By which they attain me.

11. Out of compassion for them, I take my stand in my own condition
And make the darkness born of ignorance
Perish by the shining light of wisdom.

Arjuna said:

12. You are the supreme Brahman, the highest abode, the supreme purifier,
The everlasting shining vision, the primal god, unborn, omnipresent;

13. All the sages say this of you:
The divine sage Nārada, and Asita, Devala, Vyāsa,
And now, you say it to me yourself.

14. I believe all this to be true which you tell me, O Keśava,
Indeed, O Lord, neither the gods nor the demons know your manifestation.

15. You alone know your own self by your own self, O Fullness of Vision *(puruṣottama);*
Source and Lord of Beings, God of Gods, Lord of the World.

16. You should tell me your complete divine self's manifestations
By which you pervade these worlds and exist.

17. How may I, by continuous meditation,
Come to know you, O Yogin?
And in what manifestations are you to be thought of by me, O Lord?

18. Tell me at greater length of your self's power (yoga) and manifestations; O Exciter of Men;
For I am not satiated listening to the nectar of your words.

The Blessed One said:

19. Come, I will tell you, Best of the Kurus, my self's main glories.
There is no end to the details.

20. O Guḍākeśa, I am the self at the heart of every being;
I am the beginning and middle of beings.
And the end as well.

21. Of the Ādityas, I am Viṣṇu; of lights, the radiant sun;
Of the Maruts, I am Marīci; of stars, I am the moon.

22. Of the Vedas, I am the Sāma Veda; of the gods, Vāsave (Indra);
of the senses, I am *manas* (mind); of beings, I am knowledge.

23. Of the Rudras, I am *Śaṃkara* (Śiva); the Yakṣas and Rakṣasas, Vitteśa (Kubera)
Of the Vasus, I am Pāvaka (Agni); of mountain peaks, I am Meru.

24. Know me, O Son of Pṛthā, to be chief of household priests, Bṛhaspati;
Of generals, I am Skanda; of lakes, I am the ocean.

25. Of the great sages, I am Bhṛgu; of utterances, *Oṃ;*
Of sacrifices, I am the muttered sacrifice; of things immovable, I am the Himālaya.

26. Of all the trees, I am the Aśvattha; of divine sages, Nārada;
Of Gandharvas, Citraratha; of perfect men, the sage Kapila.

27. Of horses, know me to be Uccaiḥśravas, sprung from nectar,
Of royal elephants, I am Airāvata; and of men, the monarch.

28. Of weapons, I am Vajra (Indra's thunderbolt in the Ṛg Veda); of cows, Kāmadhuk;
Of progenitors, I am Kandarpa; of serpents, I am Vāsuki.

29. Of the Nāgas, I am Ananta; of sea beings, Varuṇa;
Of the fathers, Aryaman; of the guardians, I am Yama.

30. Of demons, I am Prahlāda; of time keepers, I am time;
Of wild beasts, I am the lion; of birds, the son of Vinatā (Garuda).

31. Of purifiers, I am the wind; of warriors, Rāma;
Of fish, I am Makara; of rivers, I am the Ganges.

32. Of creations, I am the beginning and the end, and the middle also, O Arjuna;
Of knowledge, I am self-knowledge; of speakers, I am the speech.

33. Of letters, I am the letter A; of compounds, the dual;
I am also imperishable time, and the dispenser facing all sides.

34. I am all-devouring death, and the origin of all beings;
Of things feminine, I am glory and prosperity and speech, memory and intelligence and firmness and forbearance.

35. Likewise, of hymns, I am *Bṛhatsāman;* of metres, I am *gāyatrī;*
Of months, I am Mārgaśīrṣa; of seasons, spring.

36. Of deceivers, I am gambling; of the splendid, the splendor;
I am victory, I am resoluteness, I am the essence of the real *(sattva)*.

37. Of the Vṛṣṇis, I am Vāsudeva; of the Pāṇḍavas, Dhanaṃjaya (Arjuna);
Of the sages, I am Vyāsa; of seers, the seer Uśanas.

38. Of restraints, I am the rod; of those desiring to conquer, I am statesmanship; Of secrets, I am silence; of those with wisdom, I am wisdom.

39. And further, O Arjuna, I am the seed of all beings;
There is no being, moving or unmoving, which can exist without me.

40. There is no limit to my marvelous manifestations, O Conqueror of the Foe,
But I have declared this as only an illustration of my glory.

41. Whatever reality *(sattva)* has glory, majesty and power,
Understand that to be sprung from a spark of my light.

42. But of what use is this detailed knowledge to you, Arjuna?
I keep continually pervading this entire world
With only one fraction (of myself).

This is the tenth chapter, entitled "The Yoga of Manifestation" *(vibhūtiyoga)*.

Plate 4. Viṣṇu contemplating Creation, with Brahmā springing on a lotus from his navel to perform it. (From *The Hindu Pantheon* by Edward Moor, published by J. Johnson, London, 1810, and republished by the Philosophical Research Society, Los Angeles, CA, 1976.)

Chapter 11

THE YOGA OF THE MANIFESTATION OF THE WORLD FORM

Arjuna said:

1. This delusion of mine has vanished,
Due to the words you have uttered,
As a favor to me, speaking of the supreme secret called the self.

2. For I have heard in detail from you, Lotus-Eyed,
Of the arising and vanishing of beings,
And also of your changeless greatness.

3. As you say yourself to be, O Supreme Lord,
So it is.
I desire to see your form, O Supreme Vision.

4. If you deem it capable of being seen by me, O Lord,
Then Lord of Yoga, show to me your eternal self.

The Blessed One said:

5. Behold, Son of Pṛthā, my forms,
Hundreds and thousands, divine, varied in color and shape,

6. Behold the Ādityas, Vasus, Rudras, the two Aśvins, also the Maruts;
Behold many marvels not seen previously, Descendant of Bhārata.

7. Behold today the entire world of the moving and unmoving,
Standing in unity here in my body, O Guḍākeśa,
And behold whatever else you want to see.

8. But you can not see me with this your own eye;
I give you a divine eye:
Behold my godly yoga.

Saṃjaya said:

9. Having spoken thus, O King, the Great Lord of Yoga,
Hari, made visible to the son of Pṛthā his supreme godly form;

10. With many mouths and eyes, with many wonderful visions,
With many divine ornaments and many uplifted weapons,

11. Wearing divine crowns and garlands, ointments and perfumes,
Full of every marvel, radiant, infinite,
His face turned in every direction:

12. If in the heavens
There would come to be the light of a thousand suns rising together
It would be like the light of that great self.

13. There, in the body of the God of Gods,
The son of Pāṇḍu then beheld the entire world,
Divided in manifold ways, all united.

14. Then Arjuna, filled with wonder,
His hair standing on end,
His head bowed to the god and with hands joined together,
Spoke:

Arjuna said:

15. I behold in your body, O God, all the gods,
And likewise, crowds of different beings:
Lordly Brahmā seated on his lotus-seat,
And sages all, and celestial serpents.

16. I behold you, O Lord and Form of All,
With many arms and stomachs, and mouths and eyes;
And see no end nor middle nor beginning to you, O Universal Form.

17. I behold you with crown, mace and discus, glowing on all sides,
A mass of splendor, difficult to look upon,
Radiant as a sun and glowing fire, immeasurable.

18. You are the supreme imperishable,
The supreme place of rest of the universe;
You are the changeless guardian of everlasting *dharma*, the primeval *puruṣa:*
So you are to my mind.

19. I behold you who are without beginning, middle and end,
Of boundless power, with innumerable arms,
The moon and sun as your eyes, your mouth a glowing fire,
Burning this universe with your radiance.

20. This space between heaven and earth, and all the quarters of the sky as well,
Are pervaded by you alone;
O Great Self, having seen this wondrous and terrible form of yours,
The three worlds tremble.

21. These hosts of divine beings enter you;
Some afraid praise you
With hands folded together shouting "Hail!"
The hosts of great sages and perfected ones all gaze at you with magnificent songs.

22. The Rudras, Ādityas, Vasus, Sādhyas,
The Viśvadevas, Aśvins, Maruts, and Ūṣmapās,
The hosts of Gandharvas, Yakṣas, Asuras and Siddhas:
All look on you, and all are amazed.

23. Having seen your great form, with many mouths and eyes, O Strong-Armed,
With many arms and thighs and feet,
With many bellies and terrible tusks,
The worlds tremble, and so do I.

24. Having seen you touching the sky, blazing and many-colored,
With mouths open and huge eyes glowing,
My inmost self trembles,
I find no firmness or peace, O Viṣṇu.

25. Having seen your mouths terrible with tusks
Like the devouring flames of time,
I know not the directions of the sky and I find no refuge.
Be gracious, O Lord of Gods, Abode of the World.

26. And those sons of Dhṛtarāṣtra, all of them,
Together with the hosts of kings,
And likewise Bhīṣma, Droṇa, and also Karṇa,
Together with our chief warriors also:

27. They are all rushing to enter your mouths of dreadful tusks;
Some of them are seen caught between your teeth,
Their heads crushed.

28. As the many currents of rivers run towards the ocean,
So those heroes in the world of men enter your flaming mouths.

29. Just as moths with great speed
Enter into the flaming fire and perish there,
So also these creatures with great speed
Enter your mouths to meet destruction.

30. You lick up and devour with flaming mouths entire worlds from every side;
Your terrible light-rays fill the entire world with radiance and scorch it, O Viṣṇu.

31. Tell me who you are with form so terrible;
Homage to you, Best of Gods, be merciful.
I desire to understand you, the Primal One,
For your manifestation is not intelligible to me.

The Blessed One said:

32. Time am I, the world-destroyer, grown mature,
Engaged here in fetching back the worlds.
Even without you, all the warriors standing over against you will cease to be.

33. Therefore stand up, gain glory;
Having conquered enemies,
Enjoy a prosperous kingdom.
By me they are already slain;
Be you merely the occasion, O Savyasācin, (Arjuna).

34. Droṇa, Bhīṣma, Jayadratha, Karṇa, and other warrior–heroes likewise:
Slain by me, slay them, do not tremble.
Fight, you will conquer your enemies in battle.

Saṃjaya said:
35. Having heard this word from Keśava (Kṛṣṇa), Kirīṭin (Arjuna),
Trembling and with folded hands payed homage
And made obeisance to him again,
Then spoke to Kṛṣṇa, in faltering voice, afraid:

Arjuna said:
36. O Lord of the Senses, it is right for the world to rejoice and be pleased in celebrating you.
Rakṣasas run in fear in all directions,
While all the hosts of perfected ones pay you homage.

37. And why should they not do homage to you, O Great Self,
Who are primal creator, greater even than Brahmā?
Boundless Lord of Gods, Abode of the World,
You are the imperishable which is beyond existence and non-existence
And that which is beyond both.

38. You are first of gods, primal *puruṣa;*
You are the supreme treasure-house of all this.
You are the knower and what is to be known,
And the supreme goal, O Infinite Form!

39. You are Vāyu, Yama, Agni, Varuṇa, Śaśāṅka,
You are Lord of Creatures and the Great Grandfather.
Homage, homage to you a thousand times;
Homage, homage to you, again and yet again.

40. Homage to you in front, homage behind,
Homage to you on all sides, O All.
Boundless in power, immeasurable in might,
You fill all, therefore you are all.

41. For whatever I said in rashness or negligence or affection,
I have called you 'O Kṛṣṇa', 'O Yādava', 'O Comrade',
Having thought of you as my friend
And being ignorant of this greatness of yours;

42. For any disrespect done in jest while alone or with others,
At meals or in bed or being seated or when at play, O Unshaken One,
I beg forgiveness of you, O Boundless One.

43. You are father of the moving and unmoving world,
You are the object of its reverence and its greatest teacher.
There is no equal to you, O One of Incomparable Power,
How then could anyone in the three worlds surpass you?

44. Therefore having made obeisance before you and prostrated my body,
I seek your grace, O Lord;
Please bear with me, as father with son, friend with friend, lover with beloved.

45. I am delighted, having seen what was not previously seen,
But my mind trembles with fear.
Show me that other (human) form of yours, O Lord;
Be gracious, Refuge of the World.

46. I wish to see you as before, with crown, mace and discus in hand.
O Thousand Armed One of Universal Form, become that four-armed form.

The Blessed One said:

47. By my grace, and of my own self's power,
This highest form was shown to you, Arjuna,
My form composed of splendor, universal, boundless, primal,
Which has been seen before by none besides you.

48. Not by the Vedas or sacrifices or study,
Not by gifts or rites or terrible austerities,
Can I come to be seen in the world of men
With this form by someone besides you, O Hero of the Kurus.

49. Do not tremble or be bewildered,
Having seen this so terrible form of mine.
Free from fear and satisfied mind,
Behold once again this other (human) form of mine.

Saṃjaya said:

50. Having spoken thus to Arjuna, Vāsudeva revealed his own form again.
The great one, having become again the gracious form,
Comforted him in his fear.

Arjuna said:

51. Seeing this gentle human form of yours, O Exciter of Men,
I have now become composed in mind,
Restored to my normal condition.

The Blessed One said:

52. This form of mine, very hard to see, you have seen.
Even the gods are constantly desirous of the sight of this form.

53. Not through the Vedas nor austerity nor charity nor sacrifice
Can I be seen in this form in which you just saw me.

54. But by single-minded devotion *(bhaktyā)*, O Arjuna,
I can, in that form, be known and be seen in essence,
And be entered into, O Foe-Destroyer.

55. He who does my work, who has me as his goal,
Dedicated to me, without attachment and without enmity to any being,
He comes to me, O Son of Pāṇḍu.

This is the eleventh chapter, entitled "The Yoga of the Manifestation of the World Form" *(viśvarūpadarśanayoga)*

Plate 5. Kṛṣṇa. (From *The History of Hindostan*, by Thomas Maurice, 1795.)

Chapter 12

THE YOGA OF DEVOTION

Arjuna said:

1. Those devotees who attend upon you ever disciplined,
And those devotees who worship the imperishable and the unmanifest:
Which of these know yoga best?

The Blessed One said:

2. Those who, fixing their minds on me,
Worship me with constant discipline and supreme faith,
These I consider the most accomplished in yoga.

3. But those who worship the imperishable and undefinable,
The unmanifested, the omnipresent, and unthinkable,
The immovable, the unchanging, the constant,

4. Who restrain all their senses, are even-minded,
Who take delight in the welfare of every being,
They also obtain me.

5. The difficulty of those whose intellects are fixed on the unmanifested is much greater,
For the goal of the unmanifested is painful for the embodied to attain.

6. But those who, intent on me, renounce all actions in me,
Worship me with complete discipline and meditate on me:

7. These whose thoughts are fixed on me,
I become quickly their deliverer
From the ocean of death and rebirth, O Pārtha (Arjuna).

8. Set your mind on me alone,
Make your understanding at home in me;
You will dwell in me thereafter.
Of this there is no doubt.

9. But if you are not able steadily to concentrate your mind on me,
Then seek to reach me by the discipline (yoga) of concentration, O Wealth-Winner.

10. If you are not capable of such repeated concentration,
Then be dedicated to my service,
Engaging in actions for my sake,
You will reach fulfillment.

11. But if you are not capable of doing even this,
Then resorting to my own discipline,
Do my yoga and renounce the fruit of all action.

12. Knowledge is better than practice, meditation is superior to knowledge;
Relinquishment of the fruit of action is better than meditation;
From such relinquishment, peace immediately comes.

13. Without hate for any being, friendly and compassionate,
Without possessiveness or the sense of "I,"
Forbearing, even-minded in pleasure and pain,

14. The man of discipline who is ever content,
His self restrained, his resolve firm,
His understanding and mind fastened on me:
He is devoted to me and is dear to me.

15. He whom the world does not fear and who does not fear the world,
Who is free from joy and impatience, fear and agitation,
He also is dear to me.

16. He who, devoted to me, is without expectation,
Pure, skillful, unconcerned, untroubled
And who has relinquished all projects,
He is dear to me.

17. He who neither exults nor hates, grieves nor desires,
Who has relinquished good and evil, dedicated to me,
He is dear to me.

18. He who is the same to friend and enemy, to honor and disgrace,
To cold and heat, pleasure and pain,
Who is free from attachment,

19. He who is thus unattached to blame and praise,
Who is silent, content with anything,
Is homeless, of steady mind, and dedicated to me,
He is dear to me.

20. But those who have faith and are intent on me,
And follow this immortal *dharma* which I have stated earlier,
Those so devoted to me are exceedingly dear to me.

This is the twelfth chapter, entitled "The Yoga of Devotion" *(bhaktiyoga)*.

Chapter 13

THE YOGA OF DISCRIMINATING THE FIELD AND THE KNOWER OF THE FIELD

Arjuna said:
O Keśava, (Kṛṣṇa), I wish to know Prakṛti and Puruṣa,
The field and the knower of the field,
What is knowledge and what is to be known
(This stanza is not found in all the editions of the *Gītā,* so it is kept unnumbered.)

The Blessed One said:

1. This body, O Son of Kuntī, is called the field,
And he who knows it,
Those who know, call the knower of the field.

2. Know me, O Bhārata, to be the knower of the field in all fields;
The knowledge of the field and of the knower of the field:
This I hold to be (real) knowledge.

3. Hear from me briefly what this field is,
What it is like, what its modifications, and whence it comes,
As well as who he (the knower) is and what his powers.

4. This has been sung many times by sages,
In various hymns separately,
And also in the well-reasoned and definitive aphorisms about Brahman.

5. The (five) gross elements, the sense of I,
Understanding, the unmanifested, the ten senses
And one (mind) and the five sensory realms;

6. Desire and aversion, pleasure and pain,
The bodily aggregate *(saṃghata)*, knowledge *(cetanā)*, will *(dhṛti)*:
This, in brief, is the field with its modifications.

7. Lack of arrogance and deceit, nonviolence, patience,
Uprightness, service to one's teacher, cleanness,
Steadfastness, self-control.

8. Dispassion toward sense objects, lack of identification with the I,
Perception of the evils of birth and death
Of old age and sickness and pain,

9. Nonattachment, lack of clinging to son, wife, home, and the like,
Constant evenmindedness in desireable and undesireable occurrences,

10. Unfailing dedication to me and unswerving dedication to yoga,
Resort to isolated places, dislike for crowds of people,

11. Constancy in knowledge of the self,
Vision of the purpose of essential knowledge:
This is declared to be wisdom,
And whatever is other than this, is non-knowledge.

12. I will describe which is to be known,
And by knowing which one gains immortality.
This is the beginningless supreme Brahman,
Who is said to be neither existent nor nonexistent.

13. With hands and feet everywhere,
Faces and heads, eyes and ears on every side,
It stands, encompassing all, in the world.

14. Appearing to have qualities of all the senses,
Yet free of all the senses,
Bearing all yet unattached,
Enjoyer of the *guṇas* yet free from the *guṇas,*

15. Both outside and inside beings, both moving and unmoving,
Too subtle to be discerned; far away yet it is also near.

16. Undivided, yet standing as if divided among beings,
And as destroyer and producer of beings.

17. Light of Lights, it is said to be beyond darkness;
It is knowledge, what is to be known, and the goal of knowledge,
It is seated in the heart of all.

18. Thus the field, knowledge, and what is to be known has been briefly stated.
Devoted to me, having understood this,
One arrives at this state of mine *(madbhāvāya).*

19. Know that *prakṛti* and *puruṣa* are both beginningless;
Know also that the modifications and *guṇas* are born of *prakṛti.*

20. *Prakṛti* is said to be cause of the generation of causes and agents;
Puruṣa is said to be cause in the experience of pleasure and pain.

21. For *puruṣa,* dwelling in *prakṛti,* experiences the *guṇas* born of *prakṛti.*
Attachment to the *guṇas* is the cause of births in good and evil wombs.

22. The supreme spirit in this body is also called:
Witness, and Consenter, Sustainer,
Enjoyer, Great Lord, Supreme Self.

23. He who knows the *puruṣa* and *prakṛti* with its *guṇas,*
Is not born again, whatever turns his existence takes.

24. By meditation some see the self in the self by the self;
Others do this by the yoga of Sāṃkhya,
Still others by the yoga of action.

25. Others, however, without knowing this,
Worship it, having heard (of these things) from others;
And they too, taking refuge in what they have heard,
Cross beyond death also.

26. Whatever being is born, movable or immovable,
Know it to be born from the union of field and the knower of the field, O Best of the Bhāratas.

27. He who sees the Supreme Lord standing the same in all beings,
Not perishing when they perish,
He sees indeed.

28. For seeing the same Lord standing everywhere equally,
He does not injure the self through the self;
Thus he goes to the supreme goal.

29. He who sees that actions are everywhere done by *prakṛti*
And who likewise sees his self not to be the doer,
He sees indeed.

30. When he sees the various states of beings
Abiding in the One and refracting out from it,
Then he attains Brahman.

31. Because this supreme self, imperishable, without beginning or qualities,
Neither acts nor is tainted,
Even though embodied, O Son of Kuntī,

32. As the omnipresent ether is not defiled because of its subtleness,
So the self, abiding in every body, is not affected.

33. As the one sun illumines this entire world,
So does the field-knower illumine the entire field, O Bhārata.

34. They attain the supreme, who, with the eye of knowledge,
Know in this way the difference of the field and the knower of the field,
And the liberation of beings from *prakṛti.*

This is the thirteenth chapter, entitled "The Yoga of Discriminating the Field and the Knower of the Field" *(kṣetrakṣetrajñavibhāgayoga).*

Chapter 14

THE YOGA OF THE DISTINCTION OF THE THREE GUNAS

The Blessed One said:

1. I will declare still further the supreme vision, chief among wisdoms;
Knowing which, all sages have gone from this world to supreme fulfillment.

2. Having held to this wisdom
And become the likeness of my own state of being,
They are not born even at creation
Nor are they disturbed at dissolution.

3. The great Brahman is my womb;
In it, I place the seed.
From this, O Bhārata, comes the birth of all beings.

4. Brahman is the womb of whatever forms come to be in all wombs, O Son of Kuntī,
And I am the father who bestows the seed.

5. *Sattva, rajas, tamas:* these *guṇas* born of *prakṛti*
Fetter the changeless embodied one in the body, O Strong-Armed.

6. Among these, *sattva,* due to its stainlessness,
Is luminous and healthy.
It binds, O Blameless One,
By attachment to happiness and by attachment to knowledge.

7. Know that *rajas* is of passionate essence,
Is the source of attachment and craving;
It binds the embodied one, O Son of Kuntī,
By attachment to actions.

8. But the *tamas* which is born of ignorance,
Know it to be the deluder of all embodied ones.
It binds, O Bhārata, by heedlessness, indolence and sloth.

9. *Sattva* attaches one to happiness, *rajas* to action;
But *tamas,* obscuring wisdom, O Bhārata,
Attaches one to heedlessness.

10. When *sattva* overpowers *rajas* and *tamas,* it takes over, O Bhārata;
When *rajas* overpowers *sattva* and *tamas,*
And *tamas* overpowers *sattva* and *rajas,*
They also take over.

11. When the light of wisdom appears in all the gates of this body,
Then it may be known that *sattva* has increased.

12. Greed, busyness, undertaking actions, unrest, yearning:
These are born when *rajas* increases, O Best of the Bhāratas.

13. Obscurity and inaction, negligence and delusion:
These are born when *tamas* increases.

14. When the embodied one dies and *sattva* has increased,
He then attains the spotless worlds of those knowing the highest.

15. Meeting death when *rajas* prevails,
He is born among those attached to action;
Likewise, meeting death when *tamas* prevails,
He is born in the wombs of the foolish.

16. The fruit of good action is spotless and sattvic they say;
That of *rajas* is pain, and the fruit of *tamas* is ignorance.

17. Wisdom arises from *sattva,* greed from *rajas,*
Negligence and delusion from *tamas,* as also ignorance.

18. Those who abide in *sattva,* go upwards;
Those in *rajas,* stay in the middle;
Those in *tamas,* abiding in the lowest *guṇa,* go downward.

19. When the seer perceives no doer other than the *guṇas*
And knows what is higher than the *guṇas,*
He attains to my being.

20. Having gone beyond these three *guṇas* springing from the body,
The embodied one, released from birth and death, old age and unhappiness,
Attains immortality.

Arjuna said:

21. O Lord, by what marks is he who has gone beyond these three *guṇas,* distinguished?
What is his conduct?
How does he pass beyond these three *guṇas?*

The Blessed One said:

22. He does not dislike clarity *(sattva)* and activity *(rajas)* nor delusion *(tamas)* when they arise, O Son of Pāṇḍu,
Nor desire them when they cease.

23. He who, seated as if unconcerned, is not agitated by the *guṇas,*
Who thinks the *guṇas* alone act,
Who stands apart and remains firm,

24. Who abides in the self,
To whom pleasure and pain are alike,
Who is the same toward a clod or a stone or gold,
Holding equal the pleasant and the unpleasant,
To whom praise and blame of himself are the same,
Who is firm,

25. To whom good and bad repute, friend and enemy are the same,
Who has left all projects:
He is called the man who has gone beyond the *guṇas*.

26. And he who serves me with the unfailing yoga of devotion *(bhakti)*,
Having gone beyond these *guṇas*,
Is fit to become Brahman.

27. For I am the dwelling place of Brahman,
Of the immortal and imperishable,
Of everlasting *dharma* and absolute happiness.

This is the fourteenth chapter, entitled "The Yoga of the Distinction of the Three *Guṇas*" *(guṇatrayavibhāgayoga)*.

Chapter 15

THE YOGA OF THE HIGHEST VISION

The Blessed One said:

1. They speak of the changeless peepal tree,
Its roots above, its branches below.
Its leaves are the Vedic hymns.
He who knows it, is the knower of the Veda.

2. Its branches stretch below and above, nourished by the *guṇas,*
Its sprouts being the sense objects.
And down in the world of men,
It spreads out the roots that result in action.

3. Its form is thus not comprehended here,
Nor its end, nor its beginning, nor its foundation;
Cutting off this firmly rooted tree
With the firm weapon of nonattachment,

4. Then they should seek after that path from which, having gone,
Men do not return again.
(Saying) I seek refuge only in that primal vision *(puruṣa)*
From which this ancient world manifestation came forth.

5. Those who are without arrogance and delusion,
The evil of attachment conquered, established in the inner self,
Freed from desires and from the pairs known as pleasure and pain,

Who are undeluded,
Go to that imperishable abode.

6. The sun does not shine on it, nor the moon nor fire;
After men come to this, my supreme dwelling-place,
They do not return.

7. A fraction of my self, in the world of the living
Becomes a living self, eternal,
And draws into its power the (five) senses and the mind as sixth,
That come from *prakṛti.*

8. When the Lord takes on a body and also when he departs from it,
He goes taking these along,
Like the wind carrying perfume from their home.

9. He enjoys the objects of the senses,
Using the ear, eye, touch, taste and smell, and also the mind.

10. The deluded do not perceive him, whether he is departing or is staying, Or, when experiencing objects joined to the *guṇas,*
They see him who have the eye of wisdom.

11. The yogins, by striving, see him also
Abiding in their self;
But the mindless whose self is unreadied,
Though striving, do not see him.

12. That radiance in the sun which illumines the entire world,
The radiance in the moon and in fire:
Know that radiance as mine.

13. Entering the earth also,
I support all beings by my power.
And becoming the sap-natured soma,
I also nourish all plants.

14. And becoming the fire inhabiting the body of living beings
And being united with their life-breaths,
I prepare the four kinds of food.

15. And I am seated in the hearts of all;
From me are memory, wisdom and their loss.
I am the one to be known by the Vedas;
The author of the Vedānta,
I am also the knower of the Vedas.

16. There are two *puruṣas* in the world, the perishable and the imperishable;
The perishable is all beings, the imperishable is called Kūṭastha (the imperishable).

17. But other than these is the uppermost *puruṣa* called the supreme self,
Who, as the imperishable Lord,
Enters the three worlds and sustains them.

18. Because I surpass the perishable and even the imperishable,
I am the supreme *puruṣa* celebrated in the world and in the Vedas,

19. He who, undeluded, thus knows me, as the supreme *puruṣa (puruṣottama)*;
He is all-knowing and worships me with his whole being, O Bhārata.

20. Thus has this most secret teaching been disclosed by me, Blameless One;
Being enlightened to this, O Bhārata,
One will be a man possessed of understanding
And will have done his work.

This is the fifteenth chapter, entitled "The Yoga of the Highest Vision" *(puruṣottamayoga)*.

Chapter 16

THE YOGA OF THE DISTINCTION BETWEEN LIBERATING AND BINDING CONDITIONS

The Blessed One said:

1. Fearlessness, essential purity of being, perseverance in the yoga of wisdom,
Charity and self-control and sacrifice,
Study of the Veda, austerity, rectitude,

2. Nonviolence, truth, freedom from anger,
Relinquishment, peace, lack of malice,
Sympathy for beings, freedom from covetousness,
Gentleness, modesty, absence of fickleness,

3. Vigor, forbearance, firmness,
Cleanness, loyalty, absence of overweening pride:
These belong to one whose birth is of a divine condition, O Bhārata.

4. Hypocrisy, insolence, overweening pride and anger,
Harshness and ignorance:
These are the endowments of one born of a demonic condition, O Son of Pṛthā.

5. The divine endowments are said to lead to release;
The demonic to bondage.
Do not grieve, O Pāṇḍava,
You are born with divine endowments, (best circumstance for gaining freedom).

6. In this world there are two kinds of beings, the divine and demonic.
The divine has been spoken of at length;
Hear me now, O Son of Pṛthā, concerning the demonic.

7. Demonic men know neither action nor its cessation,
Neither purity nor good conduct, nor truth is in them.

8. They say that the world is without truth,
Without a foundation, a Lord;
That it is not produced by orderly complementary union,
But that it is produced by (the pursuit of) pleasure.

9. Relying on this view, such men,
Lost in self, small in mind, cruel in deed,
March forth as enemies,
Pledged to the destruction of the world.

10. Surrendering to insatiable desire,
Full of wantonness and arrogance and hypocrisy,
Holding obscure views through delusion,
These men act with impure resolve.

11. Clinging to innumerable concerns whose only end is death,
Completely dedicated to the enjoyment of desire,
They are convinced that this is all.

12. Bound by hundreds of fetters of desire,
Dedicated to lust and anger,
They strive for the gaining of wealth even unjustly
For the gratification of their desire.

13. "This I have won today; that desire I will obtain;
This is mine; this wealth will become mine.

14. I have slain that foe, and I will slay others besides;
I am lord and enjoyer, I am perfect and strong and happy.

15. I am wealthy and well-born.
Who else is like me?
I will sacrifice, I will give, I will rejoice."
Thus speak those deluded by ignorance.

16. Bewildered by many thoughts, enmeshed in the net of delusion,

Given over to the gratification of desires,
They fall into a foul hell.

17. Self-deluded, hard-headed, full of arrogance and pride of wealth,
They offer sacrifice in name only,
Hypocritically and against all the prescribed rules.

18. Taking their "I" literally, full of might, insolence, desire, anger:
These malicious men show hatred against me
In their own bodies and those of others.

19. These men, hostile, cruel, foul, the lowest of men,
I am forever hurling into demonic wombs
In the cycle of existence.

20. Having fallen into demonic wombs, these deluded ones,
From birth to death, having failed to reach me,
They go to the lowest place, O Son of Kuntī.

21. This is the threefold gateway to hell, the ruin of a self:
Desire, anger and greed.
Therefore, one should abandon these three.

22. The man who is released from these three gates of darkness, O Son of Kuntī,
Goes to the supreme destination after practising what is good for his self.

23. He who, dismissing the rules of scriptures,
Acts according to his inclinations,
Does not reach fulfillment, nor happiness nor the highest destination.

24. Therefore, let the scripture be your standard
In settling what is to be done and what is not.
Here on earth you should do the deed called for by the rule of scripture.

This is the sixteenth chapter, entitled "The Yoga of the Distinction Between Liberating and Binding Conditions" *(daivāsurasaṃpadvibhāgayoga)*.

Plate 6. Kṛṣṇa playing his flute. (From *Hindu Mythology*, by W. J. Wilkins, London, 1882.)

Chapter 17

THE YOGA OF THE THREE FORMS OF FAITH

Arjuna said:

1. What is the state of those who, neglecting the rules of scripture,
Sacrifice full of faith, O Kṛṣṇa?
Is it *sattva, rajas* or *tamas*?

The Blessed One said:

2. Born of their innermost conditions *(sva-bhāva),*
The faith of the embodied ones is threefold:
Sattvic, rajasic, and *tamasic.*
Hear about it now.

3. The faith of each man comes in accordance to his essence, O Bhārata.
Man here is made up of his faith.
Whatever faith a man has, that he is.

4. The *sattvic* sacrifices to the gods,
The *rajasic* to the Yakṣas (demigods) and Rakṣasas (demons) and the rest,
The *tamasic* sacrifice to the ghosts and spirits of natural beings.

5. Men full of the strength of passion and desire,
Full of self and hypocrisy,
Who perform cruel austerities which are not enjoined by the scriptures,

6. Who starve the collection of elements in their bodies,
And even me dwelling in their bodies:
Know that these fools are demonic in their intent.

7. But also the food dear to each man is three-fold,
And likewise the sacrifice, austerity and charity.
Hear now the distinction of these.

8. Foods increasing life, vitality, strength,
Health, happiness and joy,
Tasty, rich, lasting and agreeable:
These are dear to the *sattvic*.

9. Foods which are pungent, sour, salty,
Very hot, spicy, astringent, burning,
Which cause pain, grief and sickness:
These are desired by the *rajasic*.

10. Food which is spoiled, tasteless, foul-smelling, stale,
Which is left-over or unclean:
This is the food dear to the *tamasic*.

11. That sacrifice which is offered according to scriptures,
By men who do not desire fruits
But think simply that it ought to be performed,
Is *sattvic*.

12. Know that sacrifice to be *rajasic*, O Best of Bhāratas,
Which is offered aiming at the fruit,
And also for the sake of appearance.

13. That sacrifice is called *tamasic* which is lacking faith,
Is not enjoined by scripture, is lacking in hymns,
Is lacking in distribution of the food, and fees are not paid.

14. Honor for the gods, the twice-born, to teachers and wise men;
Purity, uprightness, continence, non-violence:
This is bodily austerity.

15. Utterance which is inoffensive and truthful,
Agreeable and beneficial, and the practise of (Vedic) study:
This is austerity of speech.

16. Mental clarity, gentleness, silence,
Self-restraint, purity of being:
This is mental austerity.

17. This three-fold austerity,
Engaged in with supreme faith by men who are disciplined
And are not desirous of fruit,
They call *sattvic.*

18. That austerity which is practised hypocritically for esteem,
Or honor or reverence,
Is called *rajasic:*
It is unstable and fleeting.

19. The austerity which is performed with foolish stubbornness,
Or with self-torture, or is done to destroy others,
Is called *tamasic.*

20. That gift which is given to one without expecting return
Just because it ought to be given,
And which is given at the proper time and place to a worthy person:
That gift is declared to be *sattvic.*

21. But that gift which is engaged in for the sake of something in return,
Or aiming at fruit,
And which is engaged in grudgingly,
Is declared to be *rajasic.*

22. That gift which is given at the wrong time and place to an unworthy person,
Without respect and with contempt:
That is called *tamasic.*

23. *Oṃ, tat, sat':* this is declared as the three-fold designation of Brahman.
By this the brāhmans, the Vedas, and the sacrifices
Were ordained of old.

24. For this reason, uttering *Oṃ,* the acts of sacrifice, giving and austerity enjoined in Scripture,
Are always carried on by the knowers of Brahman.

25. (Uttering) *tat,* the diverse acts of sacrifice and austerity
and giving
Are performed by those seeking release,
Without their aiming at the fruit.

26. *Sat* is used for the "real" and the "good," O Son of Pṛthā,
Likewise, the word *sat* is used for a praise-worthy action.

27. Steadfastness in sacrifice, austerity and giving
Is also called *sat*;
And action for the sake of these is called *sat.*

28. Whatever sacrificial offering, act of charity, austerity,
Performed without faith, is called *asat,* O Pārtha.
It is of no use here on earth or hereafter.

This is the seventeenth chapter, entitled "The Yoga of the Three Forms of Faith" *(śraddhātrayavibhāgayoga).*

Chapter 18

THE YOGA OF FREEDOM BY RENUNCIATION

Arjuna said:

1. O Strong-Armed, Lord of the Senses,
I desire to know the true essence of renunciation *(saṃnyāsa)* and of detachment *(tyāga),*
And the distinction between them, O Slayer of Keśin.

The Blessed One said:

2. Seers know "renunciation" to be the giving up of acts of desire;
"Detachment" is the relinquishing of the fruit of all action.

3. Some wise men say, however, that action is to be relinquished as evil;
Others say one should not relinquish the acts of sacrifice, giving, and austerity.

4. Hear from me the resolution of this matter of detachment, O Best of Bhāratas.
Detachment, Best of Men, has been declared to be threefold.

5. The acts of sacrifice, giving, and austerity are not to be relinquished but to be done;
For sacrifice, giving and austerity are purifiers of the wise.

6. But even these acts are to be performed, Son of Pṛthā, without attachment to their fruits:
This is my assured and final judgment.

7. The renunciation of an action prescribed is not fitting;
The abandonment of it due to delusion is declared to be *tamasic.*

8. He who relinquishes an action due to fear of bodily pain,
Performs a *rajasic* abandonment.
He does not win fruit for his abandonment.

9. He who does his prescribed action, O Arjuna,
Because it ought to be done,
Abandoning attachment and the fruit,
He is deemed to be *sattvic.*

10. The wise man, the unattached, whose doubts are removed,
Who is filled with light *(sattva),*
Does not dislike unpleasant action,
And is not attached to pleasant action.

11. It is not possible, indeed, to relinquish action altogether for an embodied self;
But he who abandons the fruit of action
Is called the detached.

12. Pleasant, unpleasant and mixed:
Three-fold is the fruit of action for the attached after death;
But there is no fruit whatever for those who renounce.

13. Understand from me, O Strong-Armed, learn of me,
These five factors for the accomplishment of all actions,
As proclaimed in the *Sāṃkhya* at the end of the *kṛta* age.

14. The seat of action (body), the agent, instruments of various sorts,
Various kinds of actions,
And (as fifth) also intention:

15. Whatever action a man undertakes with his body, speech, and mind,
Whether right or wrong,
These are its five causes.

16. This being so, he who because of undisciplined intellig-
ence,
Sees himself as the sole agent,
He is a fool, and does not see.

17. He who is free from the sense of I,
Whose understanding is not tainted,
Though he slay these people,
He slays not nor is he bound.

18. Knowledge, what is to be known, and the knower
Are a three-fold incitement toward action:
The instrument, the action and the actor
Are the three-fold composite of action.

19. Knowledge, action and the agent
Are said, in the enumeration of the *guṇas,*
To be three-fold also, according to the diversity of the
guṇas.
Listen, accordingly, to these also.

20. That knowledge by which the one imperishable being is
seen in all beings,
Undivided in the divided,
Know that that knowledge is *sattvic.*

21. That knowledge which knows the manifold different
conditions in all beings,
Because of their separateness,
Know that knowledge is *rajasic.*

22. But that which clings to one single effect as if it were the
whole,
Missing the cause, without grasping the real and nonapparent,
Is said to be *tamasic.*

23. An action which is obligatory,
Performed without attachment and without desire or
hate by one undesirous of the fruit,
That is said to be *sattvic.*

24. But action which is done in great strain
By one seeking to gratify his desires or by the sense of I,
Is said to be *rajasic.*

25. That action which is undertaken out of delusion,
Without regard to consequences, or to loss and injury, or to one's human capability,
Is called *tamasic.*

26. The actor who is free from attachment and not taking first person speech (literally),
Is without agitation in regard to success and failure,
And is filled with strength (of vision) and firmness,
Is called *sattvic.*

27. That actor who is passionate, desirous of the fruit of action,
Lustful and impure and violent,
Filled with exaltation and grief,
Is called *rajasic.*

28. That actor who is undisciplined, unrefined, obstinate,
Deceitful, dishonest, indolent,
Despondent and procrastinating,
Is called *tamasic.*

29. O Wealth-Winner, hear the three-fold differentiation of understanding and firmness also,
According to the *guṇas,*
Declared fully and separately.

30. That (understanding) which knows action and inaction,
What ought to be done and what ought not to be done,
The fearful and what is not, bondage and release,
That understanding, O Son of Pṛthā, is *sattvic.*

31. That, O Son of Pṛthā, by which one understands incorrectly *dharma* and *adharma,*
And also what ought to be done and what ought not to be done,
That understanding is *rajasic.*

32. That which, O Son of Pṛthā, covered by darkness,
Deems as *dharma* what is *adharma,*

And thinks all things in reversed fashion,
That understanding is *tamasic.*

33. The firmness (of judgment) by which one holds the workings of the mind, life-breath, and the senses,
By way of undeviating yoga,
That, O Son of Pṛthā, is *sattvic.*

34. But that firmness (of judgement) by which one, desiring fruit,
Holds fast to worldly goals, *dharma,* wealth, pleasure
In an attached manner,
That, O Son of Pṛthā, is *rajasic.*

35. That firmness (of judgment) by which the fool does not give up sleep, fear, grief, depression and pride,
That, O Son of Pṛthā, is *tamasic.*

36. But hear now from me, O Best of the Bhāratas, the three-fold happiness,
In which man rejoices by long practise,
And comes to the end of suffering.

37. That which, born of clarity in one's understanding of self,
Is at first like poison but in the end is the finest nectar,
That is *sattvic.*

38. That happiness which (arises) from the union of the senses and their objects,
Is in the beginning like the finest nectar but in the end like poison,
That is called *rajasic.*

39. That happiness which deludes the self in the beginning and in the end,
Arises from sleep, indolence and heedlessness,
That is called *tamasic.*

40. There is no actuality either on earth or in heaven, even among the gods,
Which is free of these *guṇas* born of *prakrti.*

41. The works of Brahmans, *Kṣatriyas, Vaiśyas* and *Sūdras,* O Foe-Destroyer,
Are distinguished by the *guṇas* that arise from their own inner condition.

42. Repose, self-restraint, austerity,
Cleanness, patience and uprightness,
Piety, wisdom and knowledge,
Are the actions of the Brahman, born of his own condition.

43. Heroism, energy, firmness,
Resourcefulness, and not fleeing in battle,
Generosity and lordliness,
Are the actions of the *Kṣatriya,* born of his condition.

44. Agriculture, cattle-tending, trade,
Are the actions of the *Vaiśya,* born of his condition;
Service is the action of the *Sūdra,* born of his condition.

45. A man, dedicated to his own action, attains fulfillment.
Hear then in what way he finds fulfillment,
When one is dedicated to action.

46. A man finds fulfillment by worshipping him, through his own proper action,
From whom all beings arise and by whom all this is pervaded.

47. One's own *dharma,* even when not done perfectly,
Is better than an alien *dharma,* even though well performed;
One does not incur sin doing the action prescribed by one's own condition (doing one's thing).

48. One should not abandon the action congenial to one,
Even though it is defective,
For all undertakings are clouded with defects
Like fire by smoke, O Son of Kuntī.

49. He whose understanding is everywhere unattached,
Who is without yearning, whose self is subdued,

Arrives by renunciation at the supreme fulfillment of
freedom,
From the bondage of action *(naiṣkarmya)*.

50. Understand from me succinctly, O Son of Kuntī,
How, he who has reached fulfillment, has reached
Brahman,
Which is the supreme state of wisdom.

51. Disciplined with a pure understanding,
Having restrained his self with firmness,
Having relinquished sound and other sense objects,
Casting aside passion and hate,

52. Dwelling alone, eating little, with mind, body and
speech controlled,
Constantly engaged in the yoga of meditation,
Supported by dispassion,

53. Having forsaken the sense of I, might, insolence,
Desire, anger, possession;
Unselfish and at peace, he is fit to become Brahman.

54. Having become Brahman, tranquil in the self,
He neither grieves nor desires;
Regarding all beings as equal, he attains supreme dedication to me.

55. Through this dedication, he knows me in essence;
Then having known me essentially, he forthwith enters
into me.

56. Ever performing all actions, taking refuge in me,
By my grace, he reaches the eternal, imperishable
abode.

57. Renouncing all action to me with your mind,
Intent on me, relying on the yoga of understanding.
Become constantly mindful of me.

58. If mindful of me, you will cross all obstacles by my grace.
But if, due to your sense of I, you will not pay heed,
You will perish.

59. If, having centered in your sense of I, you think "I will not fight,"
Your resolve will be in vain:
Prakṛti will impel you.

60. Tied to your own action born of your condition, O Son of Kuntī,
You will do helplessly
That which, due to delusion, you do not want to do.

61. The Lord stands in the heart of all beings, O Arjuna,
By his power causing all beings to revolve as if they were mounted on a wheel.

62. Go to him alone for shelter, O Descendent of Bhārata,
With all your being.
By his grace, you will attain supreme peace and everlasting abode.

63. Thus the wisdom, more secret than any secret,
Has been declared by me to you;
Having relfected fully on this, do as you desire.

64. Hear once more my supreme word, most secret of all.
You are greatly loved by me:
Therefore I will speak for your good.

65. Mindful of me, be devoted to me:
Sacrifice to me, do me homage:
You will come to me.
Truly I promise you, for you are dear to me.

66. Having relinquished all *dharmas,* take shelter in me alone.
I shall make you released from all sins: be not grieved.

67. This is not to be spoken by you to anyone who is without austerity,
Not dedicated and not obedient;
Nor to one who speaks against me.

68. He who will share this supreme secret with my devotees,
Having supreme devotion to me,
He will doubtless come to me.

69. None among men would do anything equally dear to me,
Nor will there be another dearer to me on earth.

70. And he who shall study this dialogue of ours full of *dharma,*
Should sacrifice to me by the sacrifice of wisdom:
Such is my thought.

71. The man who, unmurmuring and with faith, shall listen to it,
He shall be released;
He shall attain the radiant worlds of the perfect.

72. O Son of Pṛthā, have you listened to this with concentrated mind?
O Wealth-Winner, has your delusion through ignorance been destroyed?

Arjuna said:

73. Destroyed is my delusion;
By your grace, O Unshaken One, I have gained remembrance.
I take my stand firmly, with doubt dispelled;
I will do your word.

Saṃjaya said:

74. Thus have I heard this marvelous hair-raising dialogue of Vāsudeva (Kṛṣṇa) and the Son of Pṛthā (Arjuna),
Of great self;

75. By the grace of Vyāsa I have heard this supreme secret, this discipline,
Related in person by Kṛṣṇa himself, Lord of Yoga.

76. O King, each time I recall this marvelous holy dialogue of Keśava and Arjuna,
I rejoice once again.

77. And each time I recall that exceedingly marvelous form of Hari (Kṛṣṇa),
My wonder is great and I rejoice once again.

78. Wherever there is Kṛṣṇa, Lord of Yoga, and Pārtha the archer,
There surely is fortune, victory, prosperity, wise conduct:
I believe.

This is the eighteenth chapter, entitled "The Yoga of Renunciation" *(mokṣasaṃnyāsayoga)*.

Here the Bhagavadgītā-upaniṣad ends.

PRONUNCIATION OF SANSKRIT WORDS

The ancient Indian grammarians of the Sanskrit language have identified forty-eight sounds as worthy of notation, and in the script that was developed over the centuries each character represents that one sound unalterably. Hence there can be no confusion about how a particular word was pronounced, though different schools of Veda transmission show slight variations in the articulation; yet compared with the haphazard correspondence of Roman notation and English pronunciation, Sanskrit notation is extremely precise.

The sequence of the alphabet again was completely scientific. The order of letters is not the historical jumble of the Roman alphabet, which imitated the sequence of Semitic scripts, but simply the path of the breath through the hollow of the mouth from the throat to the lips, producing the vowels; through the nose, producing these vowels with nasalization; and the same breath with occlusion of the tongue to points in the hollow of the mouth from the throat to the lips, producing the consonants.

The Alphabet

a ā, i ī, u ū, ṛ ṝ, ḷ, e ai, o au
k kh g gh ṅ
c ch j jh ñ
ṭ ṭh ḍ ḍh ṇ
t th d dh n
p ph b bh m
y r l v
ś ṣ s
h
ṃ
ḥ

Vowels

a—a in America or o in come
ā—a in far or in father
i—i in pit or in pin
ī—ee in feel or i in machine
u—u in put or pull
ū—u in rule
ṛ—properly *ur*, but by modern Hindus as *ri* in river or in writ. *Ṛta (Rita), Ṛg Veda (Rig Veda), Prakṛti (Prakriti), Kṛṣṇa (Krishna).*
e—ay in say or a in made
ai—i in rite or ai in aisle
o—o in go
au—ou in loud

Consonants

Consonants are pronounced approximately as in English, except for the following:

g—g in gun or in get (always "hard")
c—ch in church
sh (ś, ṣ)—sh in sheet or in shun

When *h* is combined with another consonant (e.g., th, bh), it is aspirated: *th* as in boathouse; *ph* as in uphill, etc. The palatal ñ is like the Spanish señor (jña, however, is pronounced most often by modern Hindus as "gyah," with a hard g).

Accents

The rule of thumb is that Sanskrit words are accented in English like Greek and Latin words: stress the penultimate vowel, if that is long. Length is indicated either by a long vowel or a short (or long) vowel followed by more than one consonant, e.g., *rāma, raṅga.* If the penultimate syllable is short, stress the antepenultimate, whether it is long or short: *Mahābhārata, Arjuna* (the antepenultimates are long), and also *Aruṇa* (antepenultimate is short, as in *Herodotus, Thucydides*). The real stumbling block in the transcription, which follows convention, is that of the *c*. The *c* is always pronounced as the English *ch*, never *k*.

GLOSSARY

abhinandati: be pleased or delighted.

acala: immovable.

acintya: unthinkable as a thought.

adharma: lawlessness.

adhiṣṭhāna: the body; basis or seat, foundation, etc.

Ādityas: from the Ṛg Veda, the gods that "unbind."

adhyātmacetasā (adhi-ātma-cetasā): with your mind fixed on the supreme self.

ādhyāya (gerund of ā-dhā): sharing Brahman's viewpoint.

Agni: fire; god of sacrifice.

ahaṃkāra: literally, the I-maker. It refers to those people who take first person speech and themselves literally. The Sanskrit language provides ways of making sure that the subject appears more or less involved in the action which the verb represents.

Airāvata: Indra's elephant.

aja: unborn.

akarman: inaction.

akṛtsnavidas (a-kṛtsna-vida): knows only a part.

akṣara: the term was used in Ṛg Veda I.164 and later on in Brahmanism as a prime syllable, the indestructible unit of sound with full meaning.

ạkṣarabrahmayoga: the yoga of the imperishable Brahman.

amṛtatvāya: immortality, state of endless continuity.

anabhisneha: not attached, disinclined.

anahaṃvādī: not taking first person discourse literally. Not "I" speaking.

Anantavijaya: Yudhiṣṭhira's conch horn; its name means "unending victory."

anāśin: indestructible.

antavat: perishable.

aparā: lower condition or prakṛti.

aprameya: immeasurable, incomprehensible.

Arisūdana: "slayer of enemies"; another name for Kṛṣṇa.

Arjuna: other names used for Arjuna are Bhārata (descended of Bhārata), Dhanaṃjaya (winner of wealth), Guḍākeśa (having the hair in a ball), Pārtha (son of Pṛthā), Paraṃtapa (oppressor of the enemy).

Arjunaviṣādayoga: the yoga of Arjuna's crisis.

artha: interest; purpose, motive.

asat: "that which is nonexistant." Asat refers not only to possibilities, always present, not yet formed, but also to the dogmatic attitude people take in regards to their faith which makes the "sacrifice" (or change and integration of perspectives) possible.

aśubha: evil or disagreeable.

āsurīm: demonic.

Aśvattha: holy fig tree.

Aśvatthāman: son of Droṇa.

ātman: self. The Gītā uses the term ātman extensively, sometimes suggesting by it the "universal Self," "the real Self," etc., and perhaps more often suggesting the "individual self," the jiva, the puruṣa. Although these meanings sometimes shade off into one another in the text, it is usually not too difficult to determine the meaning by the context in which the term appears.

ātmaupamyena (ātma-aupamya): the same for oneself, or "equally in oneself."

avadhya: indestructible.

avidyā: ignorance.

avikārya: immutable.

avināśin: indestructible.

avyakta: unmanifest; latent.

avyaya: immutable.

bhakti: in chapter 12, verse 1, it is translated as devotion. One should note, however, that devotion in this chapter functions as faith since it is by this faith that Arjuna hangs on by his nails to life. The life he knew has been removed from under his feet. It is by faith in the throbbing excitement of life itself that chapters 11 and 13 are connected. Without understanding this faith, the journey of the Gītā collapses. And so the model of knowing the Gītā offers to save the human circumstance, from chapters 13 through 18.

bhaktiyoga: the yoga of devotion.

bhaktyā: devotion.

Bhārata: "descended of Bhārata"; another name for Arjuna.

bhāvanā: concentration, determination, realization.

Bhīma: Pāṇḍava warrior; brother of Arjuna.

Bhīṣma: an old warrior who brought up both Dhṛtarāṣṭra and Pāṇḍu.

brahmabhūtam (brahma-bhūta): become one with Brahman or "become Brahman."

brahmacarya: celibacy.

Brahman: There are three different meanings of this word which should not be confused. Brahman stands as the absolute ground, absolute origin of everything that appears. Brahmā, on the other hand, is the god, a particular manifestation of Brahman. All manifestations appear during the days of Brahmā, and the dissolutions of those manifestations constitute the night of Brahmā. It is upon this Brahmā that the kalpas and yugas are based. The third meaning of brahman is the name given to the highest caste in Hindu society, or to a member of this caste.

brahmasaṃsparśam (brahma-saṃ-sparśa): sharing Brahman's vision (unity of touch).

brahmayogayuktātmā (brahma-yoga-yukta-ātman): "being joined by yoga to Brahman"; vision, or to share in the way of viewing the world of Brahmin.

Bṛhatsāman: a portion of hymns dedicated to Indra.

buddhi: "intellect," "imagination," "faculty of discrimination." Indian philosophical schools generally distinguish two aspects of mental life, called manas and buddhi. Manas, or "sense of mind," is the instrument which assimilates and synthesizes sense impressions and brings the self into contact with external objects. It lacks discrimination, though, and thus furnishes the self only with precepts which must be transformed and acted upon by a higher mental function, the buddhi. This is the faculty of judgment, imagination, that which gives rise to intellectual beliefs and makes understanding possible. The buddhi can become lost by following the manas, thus absolutizing its sense interpretations, or become free by striving for an embodied vision, or firm knowledge.

buddhiyoga: discipline of understanding; means of attaining correct discrimination or intellectual insight; the concentration of the buddhi on liberation, freedom, not in the context of manas: sense interpretation.

cāturvarṇa (cātur-varṇa): four-class system; see also jāti, "caste."

Cekitāna: a warrior.

ceṣṭā: activity.

cetanā: consciousness.

daiva-āsura: literally, those "wishing to know," and those bound: they are translated normally as divine and demonic qualities. They function in the text as freeing or binding perspectives.

daivam: intention.

daivāsurasaṃpadvibhāgayoga: the yoga of the distinction between liberating and binding conditions.

death: there are two paths to follow after death: the path to the sun and the path to the moon. From the first there is no return; from the second follows rebirth.

dehin: embodied; In chapter 2, verse 13.1, it is important for the reader to notice the relation that holds between context or dharma, vision and body. It is easy to see from the very beginning how Arjuna's fear coincides with the vision of his body and other bodies as just being the small objects of the context created by the battlefield. Kṛṣṇa's way from this moment on will be to embrace his concrete human circumstance—present, past, future. In sum, the body is not a bag of skin, but a way of looking at the world which has the capacity for making one's body larger or smaller. Kṛṣṇa is the prototype of the embodied vision of his whole culture.

Dhanaṃjaya: "winner of wealth"; another name for Arjuna.

dharma: law, context, field. See, karman.

Dhṛṣṭaketu: King of the Cedis.

Dhṛtarāṣṭra: lit. "one who holds the kingdom." He is the weak and blind king of the Kurus. Though legally disqualified by blindness to be king, he held the throne. Arjuna and his four brothers—the Pāṇḍavas—were brought up in this court with their cousins the Kauravas. The old blind king could not rule, even less hold the balance between his sons and their cousins. In the "great epic," the Mahābhārata, Dhṛtarāṣṭra gave his throne to his nephew Yudhiṣṭhira (one of Arjuna's brothers) instead of to the oldest of his hundred sons, Duryodhana, a cruel and selfish man. Duryodhana conspired nevertheless to gain the kingdom and destroy the Pāṇḍava brothers, and arranged to have Yudhiṣṭhira invited to a series of dice games. Yudhiṣṭhira liked to gamble and lost not only the games but also his entire kingdom. As a result, and by the stakes of the final game, he with his brothers and the common wife Draupadī, were exiled for thirteen years. Dhṛtarāṣṭra was displeased with this venture and promised the Pāṇḍavas that after the exile and under certain conditions they could return to their kingdom and reclaim it. When the period of exile was over and the conditions met, however, Duryodhana refused to give up the kingdom. The weak king could not bring about a reconciliation between the cousins, and when both sides appealed to their relatives and friends they found themselves on the brink of a civil and family war. When the battle is about to begin, Arjuna's crisis takes place and the Gītā unfolds our own radical condition.

dhṛti: courage; will.

dhyānayoga: the yoga of meditation.

Draupadī: wife of the five Pāṇḍava brothers.

dṛdhavratāḥ (dṛdha-vratāḥ): resolutions; literally, "solid vows."

Droṇa: the instructor who taught the art of war to both the Pāṇḍava and the Kuru princes.

Drupada: the King of Pāncāla, father-in-law of Arjuna; Dhṛṣtadyumma is his son.

Duryodhana: the oldest of Dhṛtarāṣṭra's hundred sons; a cruel and selfish man.

dvandva: pairs, suggesting various opposites like pleasure and pain, cold and heat, etc. The dual compound in Sanskrit that strings words together with equal status.

dvapara yuga: a period which lasts 864,000 years.

dveṣṭi: upset; dislike, be hostile to.

gandharvas: divine musicians.

gāyatrī: meter of twenty-four syllables.

Govinda: "herdsman" or "giver of enlightenment"; another name for Kṛṣṇa.

Guḍākeśa: "having the hair in a ball"; another name for Arjuna.

guṇakarmavibhagayos (guṇa-karma-vi-bhaga): there is ontological unity between vision and action but not between the doer and the action.

guṇas: three elemental and dynamic human "systems" which and through which knowledge is made possible. Inertia or resistance (tamas), energization (rajas), and resolution toward the fully organized system (sattva) are the conditions of possibility for knowledge to be liberated from its dependence on the manas—interpretation. Thus transcendence into the buddhi—interpretation of sense objects or impressions is possible.

guṇatrayavibhāgayoga: the yoga of the distinction of the three guṇas.

hetu: causes.

Hṛṣīkeśa: "lord of the senses"; another name for Kṛṣṇa.

indriyāṇī: (the) senses: the usual five with manas (sense interpretation) sometimes taken as the sixth.

Janaka: King of Mithilā, father of Sītā, wife of Rāma. Though a king, he worked to inspire the people.

Janārdana: "the liberator of men"; another name for Kṛṣṇa.

jñāna: knowledge, wisdom; see vijñāna. The distinction between the two terms in the Gītā appears more a distinction of quality. Jñāna is closer to vision than vijñāna.

jñānavijñānayoga: the yoga of wisdom and understanding.

jñānayoga: the yoga of knowledge.

kali yuga: the "dark age" which lasts for 432,000 years.

kalmaṣa: sin, guilt.

Kalo 'smi: "I am time." Humankind is not in time. We *are* time: our own time, which needs to be remade anew constantly and eternally.

kalpa: see yuga.

kāma: desire; sensuous delights.

kāmadhuk: the wish-granting cow; a Ṛg Vedic allusion.

kāmasaṃkalpavarjitās (kāma-sam-kalpa-varjita): free from desire (kāma) and compulsion (sam-kalpa).

Kandarpa: the god of love.

kāraṇa: the mans or the cause; instrument.

karma: action.

karman/dharma: The drama of the Gītā unfolds in the way the relation between these two terms unfolds. Karman never appears by itself, but is always the concrete karman which a particular dharma gives rise to. Dharma is the particular context within which a series of actions are determined. Karmic determination becomes emancipation only when the dharma is known. The Sanskrit roots of the words karman and dharma confirm these insights. The word karman is a noun meaning action from the root kṛ, "doing, acting, performing." The root of the word dharma, dhṛ, means, "to support, sustain, hold together"; namely, dharma is the general or particular context and structure which holds together certain objects with definite and determined programs of action. Thus we have rājadharma (duties to be performed by a king), padārthadharma (the ordering of natural elements), samājadharma (the ordering of norms of a community), etc.

karman: action.

karmasaṃnyāsayoga: the yoga of the renunciation of action.

karmasu kauśalam: skill in action; the perfection which results from concentrated activity carried on without being obsessively concerned with the results of the activity.

karmayoga: sharing in that viewpoint that looks for emancipation through action.

karmendriyāṇi (karma-indriya): organs of actions; or the five "motor organs"; tongue, feet, hands, the ejective and generative organs.

Karṇa: half-brother to Arjuna.

kartā: the agent.

kartṛtva: agency.

kārya: acts or effects.

Keśava: "having fine hair"; another name for Kṛṣṇa.

kilbiṣa: sin, guilt—as with pāpa, violation of social order.

Kṛpa: brother-in-law of Droṇa.

Kṛṣṇa: other names used for Kṛṣṇa are Madnusūdana (slayer of the demon Madhu), Arisūdana (slayer of enemies), Govinda (herdsman or giver of enlightenment), Vāsudeva (son of Vāsudeva), Yādava (descendent of Yadu), Keśava (having fine hair), Mādhava (the husband of Laksmī),Hṛṣīkeśa (lord of the senses, hṛṣīka-īśā), Janārdana (the liberator of men).

kṛta: the "golden age" which lasts for 1,728,000 years.

Kṣatriyas: a philosopher/warrior.

kṣetrakṣetrajñavibhāgayoga: the yoga of discriminating the field and the knower of the field.

Kubera: lord of wealth, king of the underworld.

Kuntī: mother of the five Pāṇḍavas.

Kuntibhoja: brother of Purujit.

kurukṣetra: the field of Kuru where the battle is to take place. The significant critical point to make here is how Dhṛtarāṣṭra equates the field of battle with the field of dharma. This is significant in the following philosophical sense: to enter the battle field and to be determined by dharma are the same thing. In other words, dharma stands for the conditions or contextual situation within which certain actions must necessarily occur. In this sense, a man entering the contextual situation of war is as determined to act in that contextual situation as the weapons used in that war. It is also important to notice that the conditions that make such contextual situations (or dharmas) are man-made and, together with the objects of the contexts, carry a determination of action and a specific way of looking at the whole, but limited, situation. Arjuna's crisis arises because of the confusion in his mind between reducing life to conforming to only one kind of dharma instead of, as Kṛṣṇa will advise, integrating the different dharmas within which he functions in such a way that he becomes the complete man he is capable of becoming.

kuśa: a kind of fragrant grass.

lokasaṃgraham (loka-sam-graha): the term implied the maintenance of a human quality of human life rather than any kind of physical creation.

madbhāvāya: state of mind.

Mādhava: "the husband of Laksmī"; another name for Kṛṣṇa.

Madhusūdana: "slayer of the demon Madhu"; another name for Kṛṣṇa.

mata: doctrine.

manas: mind.

Maṇipuṣpaka: Sahadeva's conch horn; its name means "jeweled bracelet."

Mārgaśīrṣa: the first month of the ancient Hindu calendar; includes parts of the winter months of November and December.

maruts: from the Ṛg Veda, the storms.

mātrāsparśās (mātrā-sparśā): contacts with the objects of the senses of "contacts with material elements."

māyā: illusion.

mokṣa: liberation, freedom, release.

mokṣasaṃnyāsayoga: the yoga of renunciation.

nāgas: snakes.

naiṣkarmya: actionless; the bondage of karma.

Nakula: a Pāṇḍava prince; brother of Arjuna.

nine gates: refer to the eyes, ears, nostrils, the mouth, the anus and the sex organs.

nirvāṇa: extinction of desires. For early Buddhism, with which the term is usually associated, nirvāṇa was taken in its literal meaning of "extinguishing the flame of desire," or that state of being which is attained when all desire is extirpated.

niryogakṣema (nir-yoga-kṣema): not caring for the possession of property, more literally "free from acquisition and possession."

nitya: eternal.

nityasaṃnyāsī (nitya-saṃnyāsin): the eternal renouncer; one unattached in the midst of action.

niyata: that action which is prescribed by one's dharma.

niyojita (ni-yuj): compelled, constrained.

Oṃ: the sacred syllable.

Pāṇḍavas: the four brothers of Arjuna.

Pāṇḍu: brother of Dhṛtarāṣṭra, and father of Yudhiṣṭhira, Bhīma, Arjuna, Nakula, and Sahadeva. His wife is Kuntī, mother of the five Pāṇḍavas.

pāpa: sin or evil in general; in the Indian context, that which violates social custom rather than the will of a god.

parā: higher condition, or puruṣa, or para-prakṛti.

param: the Supreme, the highest.

Paraṃtapa: "oppressor of the enemy"; another name for Arjuna.

parisamāpyate (pari-sam-āp): is completed, culminated, terminated.

Pārtha: "son of Pṛthā"; another name for Arjuna.

pavitra: purifier.

Paundra: Bhīma's conch horn.

phala: fruit. This term is employed extensively in the Gītā to connote the results or consequences of one's actions; that which is produced by them.

prabhu: the sovereign Self, or "the Lord."

Prajāpati: father of creatures; appears in the Ṛg Veda and becomes most important in the Brāhmanas.

prajñāvādān (prajñā-vāda): speech of wisdom; in the context of chapter 2, verse 11.2 it means "empty rhetoric," for Arjuna has not yet learned anything.

prakṛti: original source; nature; lower condition, what manifests.

pramāṇa: standard; measure.

prasāda: clarity, serenity, calmness of mind.

puruṣa: spiritual vision, higher condition.

puruṣottama: supreme spirit.

puruṣottamayoga: the yoga of the highest vision.

Purujit: a warrior.

rajarṣaya: sage-kings who knew and ruled with the wisdom that all ways of action are enveloped by a context of knowledge. Discover that knowledge and you will liberate yourself by your own self. Vivasvān, Manu and Ikṣvāku were such sage-kings.

rajas: passion.

rājavidyārajaguhyayoga: the yoga of sovereign knowledge and sovereign secret.

Rāma: the hero of the Rāmāyana.

Ṛk: the Ṛg Veda.

śabdabhraman (śabda-brahman): rules of the Brāhmanas; the word set forth in the Brāhmanas and ritual traditions.

Sahadeva: a Pāṇḍava prince; brother of Arjuna.

Śaibya: King of the Śibis.

Sāma: the Sāma Veda.

samadarśinaḥ (sama-darśina): look equally or "see the same"; "see with an eye of equality."

samādhi: disciplined concentration, meditation.

samatva: serenity or equilibrium, evenness of mind.

saṃghata: multitudes.

Saṃjaya: the charioteer of Dhṛtarāṣṭra and narrator of the events of the war.

saṃkalpaprabhavān (sam-kalpa-pra-bhava): born of I-making; "arising from compulsion" and identification with the I-maker.

sāṃkhya system: the categories are as follows: the "gross elements" (mahābhutas), the sense of I (ahaṃkāra), understanding (buddhi), the unmanifested (avyakta), the ten senses (the five usual senses and the five organs of action), and the manas. The tanmatras or "subtle elements" are not included here.

sāṃkhyayoga: literally, "the yoga of understanding." "Understanding" literally means—and so it functions in chapter 2—as the ground upon which Arjuna stands. Only that he has forgotten. What Kṛṣṇa is going to say is no more than to throw back at Arjuna the beliefs which have held him together and acting up to this moment. These are the beliefs of his kind, on which he and all others have been acting without question up to now. Only Arjuna now forgets the ground he stands on: the memories, the promises, the beliefs, the inertia which has made him function to the point of war. Kṛṣṇa's first move is to remind Arjuna of his own ground—his concrete, though general, circumstance—what he has to save, to save himself. And it is because Arjuna has not "saved" his circumstance and has instead reduced it to the small field of battle, identifying himself with his actions that he is in crisis: in-active. If this were the case then Arjuna should not behave anāryajuṣṭam (an-ārya-juṣṭa) in a way unbecoming to his role in this context in which he so firmly believes. The first move is "memory," the first step in the path of the Gītā.

saṃnyāsa: renunciation; the giving up of actions prescribed by one's social dharma in contrast to performing these actions without attachment to their results (karmayoga).

saṃśaya: doubting; incapable of making decisions.

sāmya: equality or "non-difference," "sameness." The state of evenness of mind which follows from a strict controlling of sense interpretation by the mind, etc.

saṅga: attachment.

śarīra: body.

sarvagata: all-pervading, omnipresent, in all the worlds.

sarvasaṃkalpasaṃnyāsī (sarva-saṃ-kalpa-saṃnyāsīn): renounced all desires or "renouncing all compulsions."

Śaśāṅka: the moon.

śāstra: scripture. One must remember that the scripture in this context stands for whatever one has been taught or has heard in relation to Brahman. In many ways, it was their formal education.

śaśvata: everlasting; constant, eternal.

sat: "that which is existant." See asat.

sattva: light, wisdom, truth.

siddhi: state of arrival at perfection; determination to arrive at freedom.

Skanda: chief of the heavenly armies.

smaran: remembering. Memory plays an important role in Indian philosophy from the vajra of Indra in the Ṛg Veda to the present. It is important to notice that "to remember with one's mind" is not to live experience directly, but rather to imagine experience to be like the ghosts of memory. As Plotinus said, "Memory is only for those who have forgotten."

soma: a hallucinogenic drink used in Vedic ritual, which is extracted from a kind of mushroom.

Somadatta: King of the Bāhikas.

Somadatti: son of Somadatta.

śraddhā: the term comes from the Ṛg Veda and rather than suggesting adherence to a creed, it means the disposition and discipline to make one's life.

śraddhātrayavibhāgayoga: the yoga of the three forms of faith.

sthāṇu: unchanging.

sthitaprajñasya (sthita-prajña): one of steady mind or "one who has firmly established wisdom."

Subhadrā: son of Abhimanya, whose father is Arjuna.

śūdras: members of the fourth caste.

Sughoṣa: Nakula's conch horn; its name means "to make a great noise."

svabhāvaḥ: essence; literally, "own-being."

tamas: darkness; one of the three guṇas.

tapas: austerity. In the Gītā, the term seems to signify simply "practice," "hard-work," "effort," or "disciplined concentration."

tattvavit (tattva-vid): one who knows the true essence.

tretā yuga: a period which lasts 1,296,000 years.

tyāga: abandonment; detachment.

Uccaiḥśravas: Indra's horse.

upadraṣṭṛ: witness.

Uttamaujas: another chieftain in the Pāṇdava army.

vaiśyās: members of the third caste.

Varṣneya: Kṛṣṇa.

Varuṇa: god of the waters; important in the Ṛg Veda as the custodian of law (ṛta).

vāyu: the wind.

Veda: the Ṛg Veda.

vibhūtiyoga: the yoga of manifestation.

vijñāna: understanding.

vikarman: improper action.

Vikarṇa: third of the hundred sons of Dhṛtarāṣṭra.

Vinatā: Viṣṇu's bird.

Virāṭa: King of the Matsyas.

viṣayas: objects (or pleasures) of sense.

viṣvarūpadarśanayoga: the humanization of man, or the yoga of the manifestation of the world form.

yajña: sacrifice.

yakṣas and rakṣasas: from the Ṛg Veda, powerful binding creatures.

Yama: from the Ṛg Veda, god of death.

yatacittātmā (yata-citta-ātman): with mind and self controlled or "retraining his thought and his self."

yatani: to strive.

yathā iccasi tathā kuru: "do as you desire." Desire is the fountain of creation in Indian philosophy from the Ṛg Veda through the Upaniṣads to the Gītā.

yogayajña: sharing in that viewpoint that looks for emancipation through sacrifice.

Yudhāmanyu: a chieftain in the Pāṇdava army.

Yudhiṣṭhira: son of Kuntī; brother to Arjuna.

Yuduhāna: a charioteer, also called Sātyaki.

yuga: the cyclic history of man.

yugas: mark the eternal creation of the species. The difference between the "golden age" (kṛta) and the "dark age" (kali yuga) is just one of decline in one's self-critical attitude toward one's own conceptual schemes. Brahmā, the god, not Brahman, the ground of all possible creations, has as one of his life-days a rotation of a thousand times of the four cycles. This is called *kalpa*. Manifestations appear during the day of Brahmā; the dissolution of these manifestations constitute the night of Brahmā: the appearance of the avatāra, like Kṛṣṇa.

yukta (from yuj): disciplined.

yuktātmā: self-effort; steadfastness.

Yuyudhāna: a Pāṇdava ally.